WESTERN CAPE & COFETE ★6

A trip in an open jeep to the island's western tip and Cofete brings rally-level fun to a landscape of solitude (see photo).

Tip: The Cofete panorama from the top of the pass improves in the afternoon light. Wait for the return trip to get the best photos.

➤ p. 107, The South

SCUBA DIVING ★7

Even beginners can explore the fascinating underwater world around the island on a diving course.

➤ p. 34, Sport & activities

GUIDED ISLAND HIKES ★8

Expert guides open your eyes to the island's hidden secrets – and the stories behind them.

➤ p. 33, Sport & activities

SURFING ★9

Experience the sea, sky and golden beaches of the real Fuerte from a board on the water – try windsurfing, kitesurfing or just plain surfing.

➤ p. 35, Sport & activities

CARNIVAL ★10

Watch the fun parades and join the dancing in the heat of the night in Puerto del Rosario – you could pretend you're in Rio!

➤ p. 127, Festivals & events

CONTENTS

Plan your visit
€-€€€ Price categories
(*) Premium-rate phone number
Eating/drinking
Shopping
Going out
Top beaches
Hot day activities
Budget activities
Family activities
Classic experiences

(A2) Refers to the removable pull-out map
(0) Located off the map

BEST OF FUERTEVENTURA

Beach on the Jandía peninsula

A POET'S CHOICE

A tour of the *Casa Museo Unamuno*, the former hotel where the Spanish poet Miguel de Unamuno stayed, provides a fascinating journey into the past, and is interesting enough to visit more than once (photo).

➤ p. 62, The North

ART FOR A CHANGE

Have a look at contemporary art at the *Centro de Arte Juan Ismaël* in Puerto del Rosario – where there is also a cafeteria.

➤ p. 62, The North

INDOOR SHOPPING

The air-conditioned interior of the multi-storeyed shopping centre *Las Rotondas* in the capital Puerto del Rosario offers a welcome refuge from the scorching heat. There are 30,000m² of shops and eateries.

➤ p. 63, The North

SIGHT & SOUND

Betancuria's *multimedia presentation* showcases the most beautiful aspects of the Canary Islands with pictures and an accompanying soundtrack. A highlight is the fantastic display of flowers that appear out of nowhere after winter rainfall.

➤ p. 72, The Centre

BOWLING, BILLIARDS & MORE

The *Mega Park Family Entertainment Center* at the Centro Comercial Atlántico in Caleta de Fuste offers a varied programme of entertainment for adults and children alike in an indoor, air-conditioned setting. Try bowling, snooker and all sorts of games of chance.

➤ p. 80, The Centre

BEST ON A BUDGET

FOR SMALLER WALLETS

SURF CAMPS

Some surf and windsurf schools offer hostel accommodation for their students. While not exactly luxurious, they are unbeatably cheap and a good source of information. Best to enquire before your trip because most only have one or two dozen beds.

OPEN-AIR ART

Puerto del Rosario's *Parque Escultórico* (sculpture park) covers almost the whole of the island's capital. The city exhibits the best works from the local sculpture competition, which has been running for the last ten years. A leaflet is available showcasing 16 of these artworks (photo).

➤ p. 62, The North

CHEESE PLEASE!

A friendly smile and tasty cheese can be enjoyed at *Finca Pepe* goat farm, close to Betancuria, where you can watch the entire cheese-making process for free – from the milking of their goats to the finished block of cheese!

➤ p. 74, The Centre

VISIT THE ANCIENT CANARIANS

Even the drive through a *malpaís* – an uninhabitable lava field – is something special. Get a glimpse into just how hard life was for the island's original inhabitants when you visit the ruins of the partially restored lava huts in the ancient Canarian settlement of *Atalayita*.

➤ p. 77, The Centre

HAPPY HOUR

You'll find the classic happy hour mainly in places with a large UK contingent. In the early evening, pubs serve beer at half price or offer two-for-one deals and generous discounts on cocktails. The best deals are in *Caleta de Fuste*.

➤ p. 82, The Centre

BEST WITH CHILDREN

FUN FOR YOUNG & OLD

CAIRN COMPETITION, ANYONE?
Who can build the highest? Mum, dad, one of the kids? Both the south (near *Esquinzo*) and the north (near *Cotillo*) have all the pebbles you could need to test your skill and patience. But watch out! Frustration can run high.

UNDER THE SEA
What does the world actually look like underwater? Take a trip on a semi-submarine or glass-bottomed boat to find out without dipping so much as a toe in the water. Wait for the fish food to be sprinkled in the water for a truly magical moment. Find trips from *Corralejo, Costa Calma* and sometimes *Morro Jable*.

WITH THE BIG SURFERS
In Playitas, Lajares and elsewhere, some water-sports schools also cater for school-age children, offering paddle boarding, kayaking, windsurfing and traditional surfing. Some, like *Joyas Surf* in Lajares, even have courses for the whole family.
➤ p. 56, The North

MEET THE ANIMALS
There's nowhere better to get up close and personal with exotic animals than *Oasis Park* near La Lajita. More than the usual zoo experience and shows, the park offers special attractions such as meeting the lemurs and sea lions, and camel rides.
➤ p. 85, The Centre

OUT TO SEA
Sail out on a catamaran from Corralejo or Morro Jable with no engine noise and plenty of space on deck. For the little ones your best bet is the *pirate tour* on the *Pedra Sartaña* from Morro Jable.
➤ p. 103, The South

BEST

CLASSIC EXPERIENCES

ONLY ON FUERTEVENTURA

WIND, WAVES, WORLD CUP
The island holiday experience does not get better than when the best windsurfers in the world visit the beautiful lagoon landscape of the Canary Islands and amaze the crowds with their skills. Beach parties are the order of the day for the fortnight.
➤ p. 35, Sport & activities

"BADLAND"? SAYS WHO?
To experience the *malpaís* (best at the volcanic craters in the north) is to experience a special kind of landscape: near impassable grey-black crumbly lava as far as the eye can see. Try a guided hike or a buggy or bicycle tour.
➤ p. 48, The North

LIVING HISTORY
Delve deep into Fuerteventura's past at the outdoor museum *La Alcogida* near Tefía. The village comes to life with traditional crafts workshops (photo).
➤ p. 65, The North

FISH IN LAVA
The island has become a world-class diving destination, mainly due to the underwater lava formations which are home to all kinds of colourful fish and sea creatures, for example at *Caleta de Fuste*.
➤ p. 81, The Centre

FRESH FROM THE FIELD
Or from the artisan, at least. It's nigh on impossible to leave the *Mercado Agro-Artesanal* at Oasis Park empty-handed. They sell prickly pear jam, *mojo verde*, soap and toys; island produce is more vibrant than you might expect.
➤ p. 85, The Centre

ENDLESS BEACHES
Located above deserted beaches that seem to go on forever, *Cofete* boasts mountainous terrain with no hotel complexes to spoil the view. And there is also the mysterious Villa Winter…
➤ p. 107, The South

GET TO KNOW FUERTEVENTURA

The island's goats roam the highlands

DISCOVER FUERTEVENTURA

No it's not Mars; it's the mountainous landscape of Fuerteventura's interior

Surfing, diving, sunbathing, sailing, hiking or simply relaxing. These are just some of the favourite pastimes of guests to Fuerteventura. The island's charm may not be obvious at first glance, but this is precisely what makes Fuerteventura so special. This Canary Island is an unassuming alternative to its neighbours and, while offering many activities, is really only famous for its miles and miles of beaches.

BACK TO BASICS

Dissidents of the Spanish regime were once forced into exile on the island. The most famous of these, poet Miguel de Unamuno, called the island "... a naked, bare, barren land of bones" – but also "an oasis in the middle of civilisation's

3rd century BCE
Settlement of the Canaries begins

1st/2nd century CE
First written reference to the Canary Islands by Pliny the Elder

1403–05
The Norman, Jean de Béthencourt, conquers Fuerteventura for the Spanish Crown

Late 15th century
The Spanish Crown starts to send noblemen and priests to reign as *señores* over the locals

1730–36
After a volcanic eruption, residents from Lanzarote flee to the neighbouring island of Fuerteventura

desert" and "a country that is able to harden a tired soul". Once the most deprived among all the Canary Islands, this unpretentious island with its modest villages has definitely become an oasis for anyone looking to relax and rejuvenate their soul, provided they are willing to try what the island so generously offers. All the sun worshippers and surfing enthusiasts who now flock to Fuerteventura also appreciate this about the island: its primitive nature, its wild landscape of sand, stone and shrubs and its remote location in the middle of the ocean. It is an island that is an austere symphony of colours: white beaches, blue skies, azure waters, parched grassy plains and gunmetal boulders. You will find no hint of the lush vegetation of La Palmas or the scenic diversity of Tenerife, and nothing of the bustling city life of Gran Canaria. Fuerteventura remains one of the most sparsely populated of the Canary Islands with a population density of only 61 inhabitants per square kilometre.

A TRANQUIL LANDSCAPE

The island offers an ideal escape from the usual sensory overload. Here, the stress of sightseeing will not put a damper on your relaxation as there are neither ancient walls nor famous museums. But you should still take some time out to go on a trip or, better still, a guided hike to discover for yourself some of the island's hidden attractions – be it gorges, the lava fields or village churches – so that you can experience the spirit of the island. How about a siesta in a small fishing or mountain village? Because in the older villages one thing reigns

1837
The island's *Señorío* feudal system is abolished

1852
The Canaries become a free trading zone; a boom ensues due to the export of dye, soda ash and lime, to name just a few products

1912
The islands are granted self-governance

1966/67
Tourism arrives

1986
Spain joins the EU; the Canary Islands obtain special status

2017
Fuerteventura receives the Spain Quality Tourism Award

supreme above all: peace. There you can sit underneath a canopy of leaves in front of the village church and enjoy the hibiscus blossomsand the sunlight as it dapples the pavement, and feel as though all around you time is standing still. The landscape has a calming effect, even if it does not vary a lot: there are some volcanic peaks and deep valleys, lava beds, the occasional palm tree oasis, a handful of small, picturesque mountain villages and even fewer sleepy fishing villages. The coastline, on the other hand, is beautiful and varied: there are the endless stretches of bright fine sandy beaches of the Jandía Peninsula; the pristine white dune beach at Corralejo; the dark almost black pebbles of the small coves of fishing villages in the south of Maxorata, the main body of the island; and the wild waves buffeting the cliffs in the west.

WATER SPORTS AHOY!

This brings us to the island's main draw: the water. With its stable weather conditions and beaches with all levels of difficulty, the coast attracts a colourful surfing crowd. Beginners can learn very quickly, as it seldom rains and there are no storms or sudden downpours. If the art of surfing doesn't appeal, then you can always sail on a catamaran or try your luck with some deep-sea fishing. The true quality of Fuerteventura's sea is experienced when you go snorkelling or scuba diving; it has the most fantastic underwater world and a plethora of dive sites along its coasts. Every diving school has its own special site. These can range from the quite bizarre – like the undersea solidified lava rivers – to just clear white sand or even slowly decaying shipwrecks near the coast, teeming with fish and other sea life.

FESTIVALS

The best way to experience the authentic Spanish nature of the island is during a fiesta. This is when bands play in the town square at night and people dance; there are stalls selling snacks and young and old alike are out and about. On the main holy day, a procession of saints moves through the village, the dignitaries in front followed by the village folk in their full festive dress. Nowadays, the traditional dates are overshadowed by new tourist draw cards – the large international events which for many are reason alone to travel. This is especially true for the annual Windsurfing World Championships at the end of July or the beginning of August. In January, music enthusiasts flock to the Music Festival, and in early November during the International Kite Festival the heavens above the shifting sand dunes are filled with imaginative and colourful kites.

And when your last evening on the island approaches, how to say goodbye? Another beach party? A paella with fresh seafood in the hotel restaurant? Sangría at the pool bar? Perhaps it would be a good idea to take one last drive to a sleepy fishing village, where, on the beach terrace of a small *bar-restaurante* you can enjoy some delicious fresh fish, drink some local dry wine, listen to the sound of the breaking waves and feel the trade winds tug at your hair …

AT A GLANCE

118,000
Inhabitants

Cheltenham: 118,800

24
Number of volcanoes

As many as in Italy (incl. islands)

77km
of beaches, accounting for 24% of the coastline

Coast of Isle of Wight: 92km

1,670km²
area

Greater London: 1,572km²

DISTANCE TO AFRICA
97km

Narrowest crossing of the English Channel: 23km

HIGHEST RECORDED TEMPERATURE:
43°C

LOWEST: 8°C

TRADITIONAL FIESTAS PER YEAR
70

2,852 HOURS OF SUNSHINE PER YEAR

That's 65% of all daytime hours. For comparison: London has 1,659 hours of sunshine per year.

80,000

goats live on Fuerteventura

28%
of the inhabitants were born on the island

BETANCURIA
SMALLEST ISLAND LOCAL AUTHORITY (POPULATION: 680)

UNDERSTAND FUERTE VENTURA

A LAVA OUTCROP?

Volcanoes dominate the landscape of the oldest Canary Island, especially the distinct volcanic cones which overshadow the regions in the north and around Tuineje. But unlike its neighbour Lanzarote, which is still volcanically active on its surface, the majority of Fuerteventura has been formed by eruptions in the seabed. Nevertheless, the island is still covered in lava particularly in the north where fire and lava spewed out of vents around 10,000 years ago. The south also has grey-black lava fields which the locals call *malpaís*, or badland, due to the infertile desert terrain where only the island's goats roam the undulations looking for grass to chew on.

PIRATES, THIEVES, ADVENTURERS

In bygone days, a sea voyage was always an adventure especially in the wide, open seas without a coastline to follow. In this respect, the conquerors of the Canary Islands must have been a courageous group of sailors. Unfortunately, they were more than that: Jean de Béthencourt was a swindler and a cheat who had been forced to flee his home in Normandy. With his ferocious band of swashbuckling pirates, he invaded the island first in 1403, with the support of the Spanish king and the blessing of the Pope who saw the conquest as a religious crusade to convert the non-believers. Those indigenous Canary Islanders who escaped with their lives were then sold as slaves and forced to convert to Christianity: in other words, state piracy under the pretext of religion.

Over time, the island endured many pirate raids, especially from the British. They invaded coastal villages which is why the island's former capital, Betancuria, is cleverly hidden in the mountains (which unfortunately did not always protect the town). Houses were built from natural, locally sourced stone to make villages appear invisible – the buildings were only whitewashed after the invasions stopped. The last group of adventurers

to discover the island were of a completely different nature: Brits in search of a new idyllic holiday destination arrived in the mid-1960s and heralded the era of mass tourism. They have changed the face of the island more than all the thieves and pirates put together and have made the island what it is today.

PRECIOUS SEMI-DESERT

Fuerteventura has every reason to be proud: UNESCO declared the whole island and the surrounding ocean a Biosphere Reserve. What makes this semi-desert land quite so special is not evident at first glance; Fuerteventura has fewer animal and plant species than all the other islands in the Canaries. However, this wilderness is also what makes the island so special and fascinates biologists who study how plants have adapted to the arid conditions with only a light rainfall in winter.

In contrast, the underwater world is rich in marine life and every diving centre on the island has photos to illustrate it. Back on shore, 46km² are dedicated nature reserves. The semi-desert has another advantage: the island's tiny population means it stays really dark at night. As a result, Fuerteventura is also an internationally recognised Starlight Reserve, and you can still marvel at the splendour of the starry sky in all its glory.

DUSKY GROUPERS & BARBARY GROUND SQUIRRELS

Those who enjoy wildlife watching will appreciate Fuerteventura's barren wilderness. Hiking through the landscape you will often spot lizards before

The sky over the Molino de Tefía offers an unobscured view of the Milky Way

Despite appearances, Canary Island spurge is not a cactus

they dart into the rocks on approach. Families of Barbary ground squirrels (similar to chipmunks) also build their habitat among the rocks, and they can often be seen in places where they are fed by tourists. This species of squirrel was first introduced to the island in 1972, when a miner returning from the Sahara brought back a pair which later escaped.

The island's diverse birdlife includes ravens and white vultures, who live on carrion, and of course gulls and other seabirds, as well as buzzards that hunt for small prey. On the tranquil beaches busy sanderlings rush along the edge of the surf looking for food, while hoopoes make their nests in the valleys of the west, and the rare houbara bustards live in the dunes of the north. When there is an increase in rainfall, partridges flourish. The rather nondescript wild canary can be found here in its natural habitat.

The sea around the Canary Islands is rich in marine life and the coastal waters teem with several bass species, mackerel, plaice, eels, rays, dogfish, blue shark, sole, brittle stars, swordfish, tuna and squid. During spring the jellyfish arrive – especially in the waters on the west and the south – and a sting from one of their long tentacles can cause unpleasant burning and, in some cases, even paralysis.

DESERT FLOWERS

Typical of the semi-desert vegetation of the island is its low scrubland of yellow *lactuca* and other wild flowers. Plants that have adapted to the drought are the rosette-like succulents, the spiky euphorbia bush, as well as the agave plants which were brought in from Central America and used for the production of sisal. The prickly pear cactus was also imported from America, and this plant is the host to the cochineal beetle from which red dye is obtained. The only indigenous tree, the Canary palm, grows in the island's oases, while tamarisks grow in those ravines that have water flowing throughout the year. In February, the yellow mimosa blossom announces the coming of spring.

MAJOREROS, MAXORATA

The J and X in these two words sound identical and are the Spanish equivalent to the Scottish (or German) "ch" as in "loch". Why then, you may ask, do the islanders write *Maxorata* instead of *Majorata*? The simple answer is this is the way it has always been and this is the way it will always be! In geographical terms, *Maxorata* is used to describe the entire island except for Jandía, the peninsula in the far southwest of the island that was uninhabited until the 19th century. *Majoreros* are the native islanders (the word "Fuerteventurean" does not exist), although today indigenous *Majoreros* are a minority on Fuerteventura. The growth of the island's tourism industry has seen Spaniards come over from the mainland to work here. To meet *Majoreros*, you have to travel inland. Only those who owned land near the island's beaches have become rich from tourism; most locals do not profit from the money spent by the two million guests who visit the island each year.

TRUE OR FALSE?

IT'S ALWAYS SPRING ON FUERTEVENTURA

So, it's never too hot or too cold? Not quite. When the hot desert wind Calima blows, temperatures can rise to over 40°C, while cold snaps in winter or early spring can bring daytime highs of 17°C and a brisk wind. At these times, you'll want a warm sweater and long trousers.

FUERTEVENTURA IS A TROPICAL ISLAND

This is the work of marketing pros wanting to conjure images of distant sun. Luckily, they got it wrong! It might never be cold in the tropics, but it rains for days on end, malaria mosquitoes abound and you always have to keep an eye out for poisonous snakes. Here, in trade wind territory, you'll get none of that! Rain showers rarely last more than a few minutes, you can skip the extra vaccinations, and a snake bite is more than unlikely. That said, don't expect to lounge in the shade of a coconut tree. The beaches on most of the island, are totally shadeless. After all, the nearest mainland coast is the Sahara!

CELEBRITY STATUS

Who is the most famous *Majorero*? Unfortunately for the island's government, the names of famous people born on Fuerteventura do not ring a bell with many visitors; for example, the writer, painter and art critic Josefina Plà (1903–99) who anyway emigrated to Paraguay in 1926. However, over the years the island has provided a second home to many famous figures. The poet Miguel de Unamuno was exiled to the island under the Franco regime, and today the island's largest statue is dedicated to him. The occasional movie star can also be spotted on Fuerteventura: the charred and eerie landscape has been an attraction for movie directors to shoot their films on the island. Sir Ridley Scott set his biblical movie *Exodus* here, while Fuerteventura was also used as a backdrop by Sacha Baron Cohen for his movie *The Dictator*, as well as for the action movies *Fast & Furious 6* and *The Invader*. Germany's chancellor Helmut Kohl vacationed here and raved about Fuerteventura's tomatoes, and Morro Jable's beach promenade honours former German chancellor Willy Brandt, who rode a donkey here in 1972 and is reported to have said: "A political equilibrium is defined by not falling off."

SAFE HAVEN FOR SEA TURTLES

Cofete beach was a hive of activity when her Majesty Queen Sofía of Spain travelled here in person closely followed by an entourage of journalists, TV cameras and the island's VIPs – and all in aid of a group of baby turtles. These small creatures were to make amends for ecological damage that once caused their extinction at Cofete beach. Known among biologists as loggerhead sea turtles, these reptiles used to come on land here to bury their eggs in the warm sand and wait for them to hatch in the sun. To turn the beach into a breeding ground for these creatures again, the first turtle eggs were imported from the Cape Verde Islands in 2009, hatched on Fuerteventura and after weeks of feeding and care (to prevent the tiny turtles from being killed by predators), the turtles were released onto the beach under the auspices of Her Majesty the Queen. The same procedure is carried out every year, but without a royal escort. Conservationists are now waiting for the first turtles to return to the Playa de Cofete for breeding when they have reached adulthood and sexual maturity.

GOATING AROUND

With the exception of insects, goats are the most common species of animal you'll see on Fuerteventura. There are about 80,000 of them on the island and, as you can imagine, they contribute significantly to the local economy. Goat farming is a mainstay of the island's agriculture since the land is difficult to farm and profits are marginal. The goats roam freely on their own or in herds in search of grass, preferring the sparsely populated regions on the rocky lava fields. This overgrazing has prevented revegetation and the island's semi-desert landscape can be attributed to humans or, more precisely, goats.

Although the majority of goats stay in close proximity to the farms where they are fed and milked daily, others are left to roam the island for months at a time and are only rounded up once a year in the autumn *apañada*. The meat from these goats (an apology to any vegetarians reading) tastes extremely succulent and is often barbecued. However, dairy goats are more important due to the milk they produce, from which the delicious goat's cheese is made. Despite the establishment of modern dairies, cheese is still made according to traditional methods. Goat's cheese is also the perfect souvenir to take the taste of Fuerteventura back home with you.

CONSTANT DRIPPING

There is a real water shortage on the island. It rains way too seldom, and when it does, eight-tenths of the water run straight off into the sea. Even before the introduction of water-pumping windmills (imported from the USA in the 19th century), when the water table was not that low, it was necessary for the locals to be prudent with their precious water resources. Fields were terraced, water collection tanks were installed on the slopes and domestic cisterns built. The water collected in the cisterns still had to be processed so that it would be fit for drinking; today limestone filtration ponds can be seen in some of the island's museums. Groundwater was hauled (and still is) from brick wells *(pozos)*, either by windmills or by animals turning the capstan wheel. This water is also stored in enclosed reservoirs but is mostly used for irrigation or as drinking water for livestock. Today, because of tourism, the increased water need is met by the desalination of seawater. Not all homes on the island are connected to the mains, with many still having their drinking water delivered by a tanker.

Handmade: the local goat's cheese

EATING SHOPPING SPORT

Never far from the sea: restaurant in Morro Jable

SAAVEDRA CLAVIJO
Restaurante
RESTAURANTE LAJA
Especialidad
Pescado

EATING & DRINKING

Pizza? Or maybe Chinese? Or just good old sausage and chips! The fact is, this European holiday paradise offers pretty much all that at almost any resort. So, nothing special then? Wrong. Why not try Spanish food or, even better, Canarian? After all, the whole point of travel is to try new things, right?

IMPORTED DELIGHTS

Eating Canarian means avoiding imported products, which always take a detour via Gran Canaria, meaning they're never really fresh anyway. But without imports, you'd struggle to prepare a full dinner. Even if the island was once known as the Canaries' breadbasket, the people here have never exactly lived in the land of milk and honey. The lack of rain means you get little yield for a lot of graft. No wonder then that most of the fields lie fallow today. After all, food has never been so plentiful thanks to the EU agricultural market, with pizza and pasta commonplace, as well as the Chinese and Indian restaurants that arrived with the British alongside a dash of Greek, Mexican and even German.

CANARIAN

Fresh food from the island is on the rise. Potatoes and tomatoes are certainly not all the island's remaining farmers have to offer. Fuerteventura's goat's cheese continues to win medals, even as the product's shape and texture have remained traditional. The menus always have a wide selection of freshly caught fish and if you stick to the local food, you will not only get fresh ingredients but also excellent value for money. However, there is one prerequisite: you have to like garlic as it is used very liberally in most dishes. Unfortunately, the most

Fish with *papas arrugadas* (left), goat's cheese with paprika (right)

typical of the island's dishes can seldom be found in today's restaurants: *gofio*, which is made from grain (often barley) that has been roasted and ground. The resulting flour is then made into porridge. This has been an island staple dating right back to its indigenous inhabitants. These days, gofio is still on sale at organic markets or in shops that sell it, for example, in biscuit-form or coated in chocolate.

WRINKLY POTATOES & MOJO

By far the most popular dish on Fuerteventura are the "wrinkly potatoes" *(papas arrugadas)*. Small, unpeeled potatoes are boiled in salty water until the salt evaporates and the salt settles in the skin. *Papas arrugadas* are normally served with fish and *mojo sauce* and often with a tomato and onion salad. The main ingredients for *mojo* sauce are garlic, red pepper, salt, vinegar and oil mixed with a variety of herbs. This makes up the red version *(mojo rojo)*; the spicy red version *(mojo picón)* is made with red chillies while the green *mojo* sauce *(mojo verde)* has parsley and coriander instead and tastes great with more delicate fish.

FISH & MEAT

The fresh fish on offer changes according to the catch of the day. On good days you'll find *vieja*, a species of the parrot fish, and on even better days there'll be *mero*, fresh dusky perch. Fresh tuna *(atún)* and squid *(calamares)* are more common. If you feel like ordering other seafood, you should bear in mind they are mostly imported frozen products. Typical fish dishes are the *sancocho* (fish with potatoes and goat's cheese) and the *sopa de pescado* (fish soup). Meat dishes are limited to goat kid (*cabrito* – depending on the season), mutton

A refreshing gin cocktail

(carnero), pork *(cerdo)* and rabbit *(conejo)*; during the hunting season wild rabbit *(conejo salvaje)* is sometimes available.

TAPAS

These days, the small Spanish sharing plates need no introduction. Here, the Canaries have made them their own. Portions are usually generous, even for a couple. Your best bet is to choose half portions *(medias raciones)* for more variety. The best Canarian tapas are wrinkly salted potatoes and goat's cheese *(queso de cabra)*, which come in cones and are also a popular starter. Other tapas from the mainland include chorizo and serrano ham.

SOMETHING TO DRINK

Wine is mostly imported from Spain and almost always dry but look out for wine from Lanzarote as well. Spanish brands also dominate the island's sparkling wine *(cava)* and brandy. Mineral water is always served in bottles, either *con gas* or *sin gas* – sparkling or still. The choice of beers on offer has improved and you'll even see some special beers from Canarian microbreweries. Cocktails, especially gin and tonic in all the variations you could dream of, are also widespread. An espresso or *café solo* is a good end to a great meal. You can also order a *café con leche* (with a lot of milk) or a *cortado* (with some milk).

RESTAURANTS & MEALTIMES

Restaurants are usually not very cheap and of middling quality and only the Italian and Asian restaurants and a few gourmet establishments offer vegetarian dishes. Most restaurants, even those seldom frequented by tourists, have menus in English, although the waiters may not speak the language. Although service is included in the price, you may still want to add five to ten per cent to the bill if you've had attentive service. Payment is made as a group, but you can split the amounts yourselves if necessary. In the Canaries, as everywhere in Spain, meals are enjoyed in the afternoons and in the evenings a little later than what you may be used to. But in the large holiday resorts, hotels and clubs, mealtimes are kept at times more suited to the foreign tourist.

TODAY'S SPECIALS

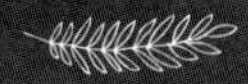

Tapas/Starters

PAPAS ARRUGADAS
Wrinkly salted potatoes, usually served with red *mojo* sauce

ALBÓNDIGAS
Meatballs

PIMIENTOS DE PADRÓN
Small green peppers, sautéed and sprinkled with coarse sea salt; mild to spicy

QUESO DE CABRA
Local goat's cheese

Fish & Seafood

CHERNE
Wreckfish, filleted (very few bones)

GALLO
Relatively firm fish with few large bones (rarely on the menu)

PULPO A LA GALLEGA
Galician-style octopus, boiled and served with potatoes

LANGOSTINOS
Grilled king prawns

PESCADO FRESCO
Fresh fish – the daily catch; the addition of "S/P" (*según precio*) means according to the daily price

SANCOCHO
Fish dish prepared with potatoes, sweet potatoes, onions and smoked goat's cheese

Meat

CABRA/CABRITO
Goat or kid; the latter is a seasonal dish and must sometimes be ordered in advance

SOLOMILLO DE TERNERA
Veal steak

Drinks

CERVEZA
Beer; choose Tropical or Dorada for a real Canarian beer; both go down well

RON MIEL
A glass with a measure of rum and some honey, sometimes topped off with a little whipped cream

SHOPPING

The Canaries are a free trading zone, but this does not necessarily mean you'll pay less, as goods are not entirely duty free and transport and storage costs are high. In fact, you may even pay more for certain items than you would back home. However, tobacco and alcohol are still very cheap.

ALOE VERA & COSMETICS

There are large plantations of aloe, the lily of the desert, on the island. The plant has well-known healing properties and there is a thriving industry of aloe vera products including ointments and natural cosmetics. The products are available all over the island but do remember that goods are perishable so don't stock up too much. Brand-name cosmetics are usually a little cheaper on the island than at home.

CLOTHING & SHOES

There are numerous casual holiday-wear brands to choose from: While Cabrito and Fuerte sell clothing with goat prints, Extreme Animals use a goat's skeleton as their symbol; *Clean Ocean Project* is an ecological brand of clothing based on the island. There is also a wide range of traditional, stylish and inexpensive Spanish shoes.

ARTS & CRAFTS

The variety of arts and crafts available on the island has grown significantly alongside the traditional selection of authentic products, and become increasingly more creative and contemporary in design. One of the most popular souvenirs of the island is white openwork embroidery. Woven palm-leaf baskets and goods are made in the open-air museum *La Alcogida* in Tefía, but it is a dying trade. Lajares is the place to go if you are

Aloe vera (left), openwork embroidery (right)

looking for more contemporary souvenirs, including ceramics, gold jewellery, silk painting, felts, extremely stylish canvas handbags. You will also find black lava jewellery at the crafts fairs held in Corralejo *(Thur, Sun)*, Lajares *(Sat)* and Cotillo *(Fri evening)*.

LOCAL PRODUCE

Popular items are prickly pear jam and goat's cheese; the latter is sold in four stages of maturity, the firmest being *curado*. There is also red cheese rubbed with paprika and the small round *queso de cabra* cheese wheels which keep very well. Jars of tasty *mojo* sauce are widely available.

LIQUOR

Brands from the Spanish mainland are well represented and Spanish brandy is good and affordable. Craft shops sometimes also sell local cactus liqueur and *ron miel*, rum with honey.

WEEKLY MARKETS

The mainly African markets that alternate between Morro Jable, Costa Calma, Caleta de Fuste and Corralejo are popular for sunglasses, bags, leather belts, T-shirts, slippers and the like, and also for African carvings. Remember to haggle! But avoid buying any fake brand names as you could get into trouble with the law back home. A special memento of your holiday is to have your hair braided with colourful pearls and beads.

The farmers' market *La Biosfera* is full of local products sold directly by the supplier *(Sat 9am–2pm | upper floor of the bus station in Puerto del Rosario)*. A similar market is the *Mercado Agro-Artesanal* in the *Oasis Park* in La Lajita *(Sun 9am–2pm)*.

SPORT & ACTIVITIES

Whether you like swimming or strolling along beaches, Fuerteventura provides all-inclusive sport and relaxation for everyone above and below the surface. If this is not enough, the island has plenty more to offer, especially for those wanting to try out water sports.

The term "large holiday resorts" refers to: Corralejo, Caleta de Fuste, Costa Calma/La Pared and Jandía Playa/Morro Jable.

CYCLING & MOTORCYCLING

Cycling has become very popular and there are rentals available at all the large holiday resorts as well as Las Playitas. They often also have organised mountain-bike trips with varying degrees of difficulty, most of them are not too demanding – you can be motor powered uphill and then freewheel downhill if you want. Racing cyclists fly out to the island to train in the winter months. If you prefer to experience the island under your own steam, you should avoid the main roads where possible. A bicycle network is currently under construction. Helmets are compulsory outside built-up areas and the alcohol limit also applies to cyclists.

Motorcycle trips with dirt bikes or quad bikes are also available in all the large holiday resorts.

FISHING

Motorboat trips for off-coast fishing or deep-sea fishing depart from Corralejo and Morro Jable but can be booked elsewhere with transfer from/to your hotel. The operators provide the equipment and offer discounts to non-fishing passengers.

GOLF

While growing and cultivating huge green lawns in a semi-desert is

Extreme stand-up paddle boarding

perhaps left of field environmentally speaking, the island's government wanted to ensure high-quality tourism. The golf course investors came just in time... but it didn't turn out to be as high-quality – read pricey – as they'd hoped. Golf on Fuerte is by no means a hobby for the wealthy elites alone, and the island's four 18-hole courses also cater to younger and less well-off players. Two are located next door to each other at Caleta de Fuste while the others are *Jandía Golf* (near Jandía Playa), and *Las Playitas* (part of the sports centre *Playitas Grand Resort*). If you prefer to start small, there is also the *golf academy (tel. 616 24 94 59)* in La Pared, where you can learn how to play golf with Irish pro Ken Ellis. There is a six-hole course and a driving range. Holiday clubs and some hotels also provide driving ranges and putting greens.

HIKING

For anyone who is interested in nature and the traditional lifestyle of the islanders, the island interior has some interesting surprises. The hike through the Barranco de las Peñitas is described under Vega de Río de las Palmas (see p. 75 and p. 119), so you can easily manage it on your own. However, it gets really exciting when you take a ★ ⚑ *guided hike* with an English-speaking guide and go off the beaten track. There's a lot more to discover than you'd ever imagine when you drive around the island, whether that be the island's primeval landscapes, the strange plants or the animals. Plus, the islanders' stories bring the details even more to life. *You can book at the travel agents in the hotels or go direct, for example with Fuerte Authentic Tours | tel. 617 69 40 67 | fuerte-authentic-tours.com).*

If you want to walk without a guide, the beaches of Jandía are a good option and are especially beautiful in the morning when the tide is going out and the wind and waves have erased the footprints of the previous day's visitors. You might even imagine the beaches to be yours and yours alone. If over the hills or through the *barrancos* are more your thing, it's a good idea to check the route on Google Earth beforehand and avoid setting off for long tours in the afternoon. Once it gets dark and without the moon it can be a struggle to make any progress even with a torch.

HORSE RIDING

The German-run stable *Rancho Barranco de los Caballos* (see p. 96) near La Pared offers rides out to the rugged west coast – giving you a true feeling of Fuerteventura adventure and freedom. In the north, the *Granja Tara* stables (see p. 54) is similar, while at Caleta de Fuste, you should contact *Crines del Viento (northern town exit in Triquivijate | tel. 678 21 31 08 | crinesdelviento.com).*

SAILING

You can learn to sail on catamarans at the *Club Aldiana* at Jandía Playa, the *Robinson Clubs* of Esquinzo and Jandía Playa, in Tarajalejo and in Las Playitas. If you just want to relax on a yacht, it can be arranged in Corralejo, Morro Jable/Jandía Playa as well as Caleta de Fuste. For skippers, there are yacht marinas in Caleta de Fuste, Corralejo, Gran Tarajal, Morro Jable and Puerto del Rosario.

SCUBA DIVING

★ *Scuba diving* on Fuerteventura is a lot of fun and dive sites such as El Río straits at Corralejo, the moray eel reef in front of Jandía Playa and various other spots are all popular. The island's lava formations and abundance of fish make it one of the best diving areas in the Canaries. Scuba diving schools are based in all the large holiday resorts as well as in Tarajalejo and Las Playitas. To learn to dive you first need a medical certificate but there are a number of local doctors who provide this service. Ask at the diving schools.

TENNIS

Good hotels and clubs have artificial grass and clay courts with wind protection, but others may only have concrete courts or insufficient protection from the wind. Lessons are offered in various hotels in the south by *Matchpoint Sports (tel. 928 54 43 07 | matchpoint-world.com).*

WATERSKIING, JET SKIING & BANANA BOATS

Jet skis are little more than floating motorbikes and are sadly just as noisy. At around 100 euros for 40 minutes, the speedy ride across the water doesn't come cheap. Companies that offer jet skis often also rent out banana boats which are towed along behind a motorboat at high speed. There are jet ski companies in all the large holiday resorts. Some of them also offer waterskiing or paragliding.

There's plenty to discover below the surface of Fuerteventura's coast

WINDSURFING & SURFING

★ *Surfing* is *the* sport on the island. The wind and water conditions are ideal all year with the strongest wind blowing during the summer. The lowest wind speeds – with occasional lulls – are from November to January. The most important spots are the Playas de Sotavento on the Jandía peninsula, the area around Corralejo and – only for the experts – the beaches in El Cotillo. Surf schools and equipment rentals can be found in all the large holiday resorts.

Kitesurfing is also a very trendy sport and popular spots are Corralejo's dune beach as well as Playa Barca in the south. Nearly all surf stations also offer stand-up paddle boarding (SUP). Windsurfing beginners have it best in the south.

Surf sites for regular surfboarders are along the west coast, in the north and on the north coast. There are surf companies in Lajares *(e.g. Joyas Surf | tel. 616 08 45 09)* or in Costa Calma/ La Pared *(Waveguru | tel. 619 80 44 47)*.

In July, surfing fanatics descend on the island for the *Surfer World Cup* – a 14-day-long party!

INSIDER TIP **Buy one get one free**

Combine learning Spanish and surfing at *Spanish and Surf (spanishandsurf.net)* in Corralejo. So while your body takes a rest your brain can get busy with a Spanish conversation course.

REGIONAL OVERVIEW

OCÉANO

ATLÁNTICO

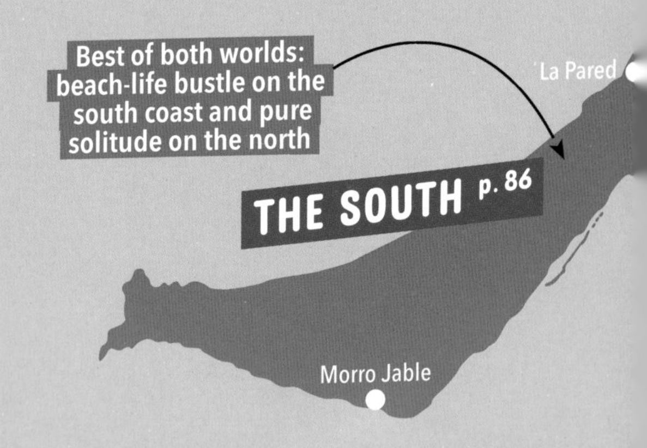

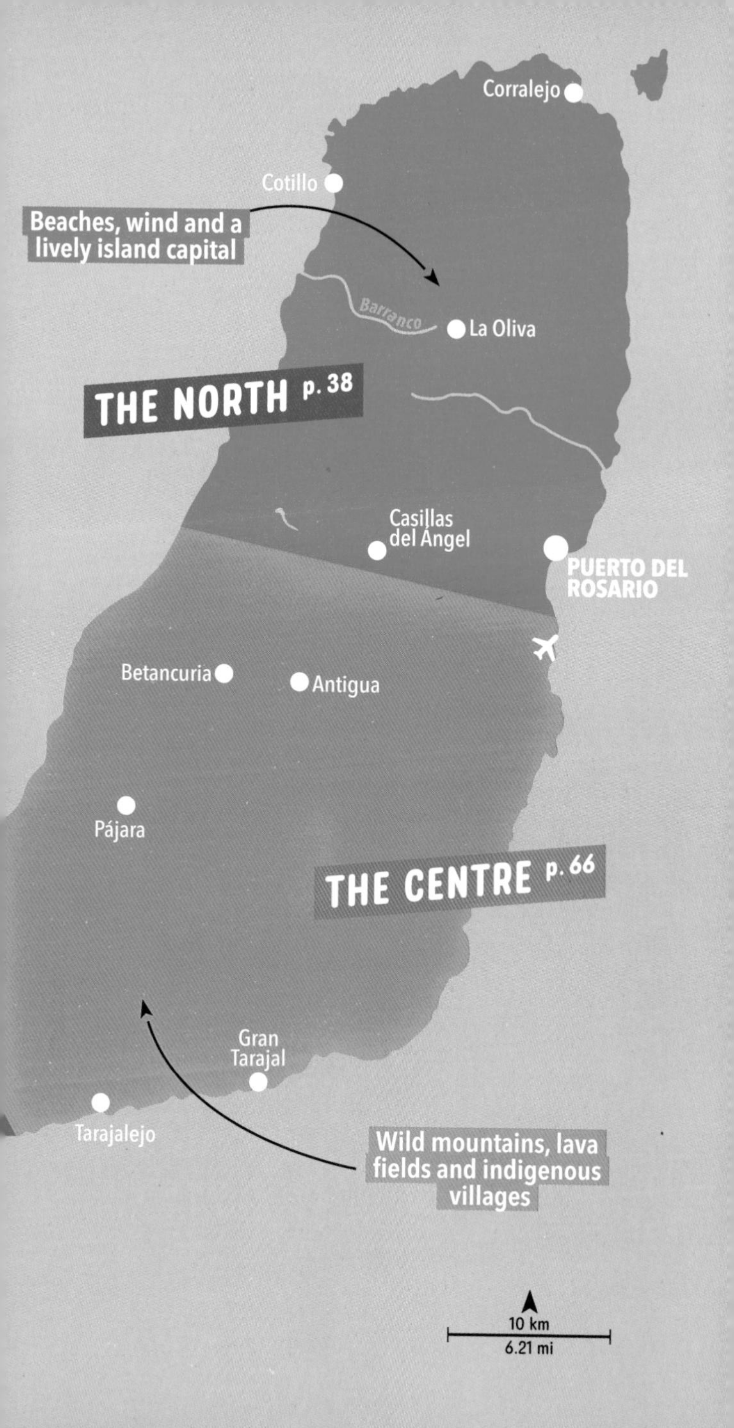
Corralejo
Cotillo
Beaches, wind and a lively island capital
Barranco
La Oliva
THE NORTH p. 38
Casillas del Ángel
PUERTO DEL ROSARIO
Betancuria
Antigua
Pájara
THE CENTRE p. 66
Gran Tarajal
Tarajalejo
Wild mountains, lava fields and indigenous villages
10 km
6.21 mi

THE NORTH

DUNES, VOLCANOES & WAVES

Even after repeated visits, it will always be an unforgettable experience: that first glimpse of the sand dunes of El Jable. Suddenly, a white dream world opens up before you with mountains and valleys of shifting sands as far as the eye can see. This is certainly the most impressive landscape on the whole island.

The north also has some other unusual landscapes, with row upon row of extinct volcanoes lining up in beautiful symmetry. Black lava

Dunes in Corralejo Nature Park

rocks are strewn over vast desolate areas called *malpaís* ("badland"), while further south the landscape is a study in russet and red; especially when the low sun catches it with breathtaking intensity. Corralejo, on the island's northern tip, is the centre of tourism. Recently, Cotillo has been developed for tourism while partly retaining its traditional character. La Oliva is one of the five historical main towns; Puerto del Rosario, the island capital, is not very touristy and underrated as a tourist destination.

THE NORTH

MARCO POLO HIGHLIGHTS

★ **EL JABLE SHIFTING DUNES**
White sand as far as the eye can see – towering sand dunes that are constantly on the move ➤ p. 42

★ **NIGHTLIFE WITH SEA VIEWS**
Things heat up in Corralejo when the sun goes down ➤ p. 49

★ **ISLA DE LOS LOBOS**
The small black lava island off Corralejo is a protected nature reserve ➤ p. 51

★ **ECOMUSEO LA ALCOGIDA**
An outdoor museum in Tefía demonstrating how the islanders once lived and worked ➤ p. 65

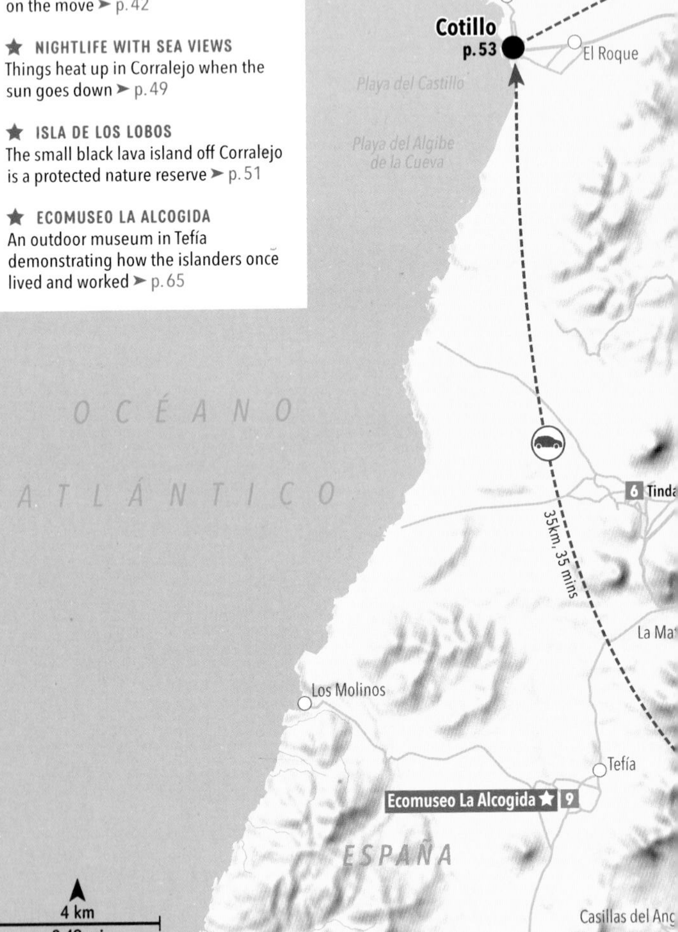

3 Lanzarote
2 Isla de los Lobos
Oasis
Nightlife with sea views
Playa de Corralejo
Corralejo
p. 42
19km, 20 mins
Playa de Corralejo
El Jable shifting dunes
FV-1
5 Lajares
1 Cueva del Llano
31km, 25 mins
FV-1
La Oliva
p. 57
Caldereta
7 Vallebrón
Majada del Caballo
El Time
Guisguey
8 Tetir
Puerto del Rosario
p. 60

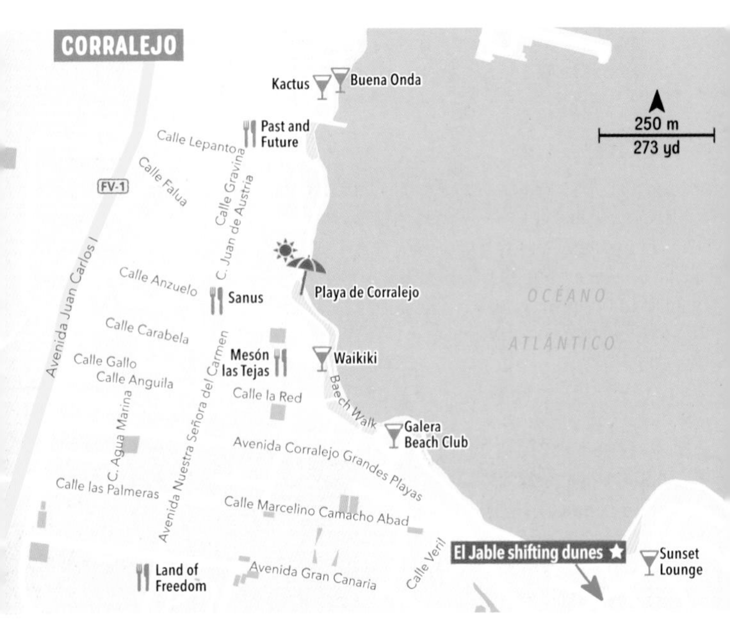

CORRALEJO

(◫ G2) **The main tourist attraction in the north owes its appeal to the 20km² dune area of El Jable on its southern edge, which merges seamlessly into the beach.**

Despite being confusingly referred to as a village in holiday brochures, *Corralejo* has long since outgrown this status. Its vibrancy, diversity and international vibe are second to none on the island. The town consists of a densely populated core which is mostly inhabited by Spanish people and a wide belt of hotels and apartment complexes that expands to the south and the east.

It has only been settled since the 19th century. In 1940, it was a small fishing village consisting of only 12 houses and when the first holiday apartments were built in 1967, the town had neither water nor electricity. The main road and the pedestrian zone, with its many shops and restaurants, form the urban centre and at night the atmosphere is exuberant. A promenade along the shore was a spontaneous rather than planned project where visitors can now eat and drink.

Apart from the Playas de Sotavento in the south, the ★ *El Jable shifting dunes* are the main highlight of the island. The white sand dunes are constantly shifted by the northeast trade winds and, with their green flora valleys and rare animals, they have formed their own precious ecosystem. The area was declared a protected nature reserve in 1982, but by then a part of the northern edge had already been developed. The biggest sin was the construction of two large hotels, *Tres Islas* and *Oliva Beach*, on the most pristine part of the dunes. Although it was later proven that the buildings were constructed illegally on communal land, the owner (the Ríu hotel chain) in 2008 still managed to obtain licenses for the hotels to trade: 10 years for *Oliva Beach* and 30 years for *Tres Islas*, with the licence for the former since extended. Progress would at least be made if the road through the dunes were closed, as once planned. But the locals fiercely oppose this measure, which is actually now overdue since the motorway has been opened. Please be aware that driving on the dunes is strictly prohibited.

EATING & DRINKING

Nowhere else on the island will you find as many restaurants with sea views, as on the narrow pedestrian promenade with the rather grand name of Avenida Marítima. *Marquesina (€€)* on the small pier has a solid reputation, and their delicious seafood crêpes deserve a special mention, as does the half-covered terrace. You can choose your own fish at the chilled counter, something that the other venues in the area also offer. There are generally only small differences in the quality and pricing of the restaurants so you can't go far wrong; just don't expect very personal service. Heading northwards (towards the harbour) you will find *El Sombrero (evenings only, closed Wed | tel. 928 86 75 31 | €€)*, who specialise in meat dishes. The interior, decorated in colourful cow hide, is a landmark in itself, as are some of the dishes, most notably the highly popular "pirates' gallows". Their neighbour, *El Anzuelo (tel. 928 53 66 26 | €€)*, is the finest and most acclaimed fish restaurant in town, with splendid cuisine and sea view through glass walls. *El Sombrero*

At the beach in Corralejo

Corralejo town beach is a great spot to watch the world go by

and *Anzuelo* also offer the option to sit outside right on the shore, although the wind often makes this difficult. The best tapas are served close by at *Tapas Oscar (closed Tue | C/ Iglesia s/n | tel. 928 86 63 88 | €€)*. Ignore the less than elegant name and take a wide selection of the half tapas portions *(media ración)*. The best pizzeria in town can also be found here: *Big Wave (evenings only | closed Tue | C/ Jesús Machín Santana 8 | €)*. The menu has three categories: classic, gourmet and white (no tomato base) pizza. Prices are reasonable and the wine is good value too.

The bars and restaurants become less touristy and cheaper the further you venture from the promenade. The tapas bar *Casa Domingo (Plaza Patricio Calero 31 | tel. 674 11 01 80 | €)* offers great value for money with its three-course daily menu and eye-catching exterior (fruit and greenery) and interior (maritime) design. Cheaper still is the self-service Italian restaurant *Da Uli (C/Crucero Baleares)* which will happily fill you up for all of 7 euros.

It wouldn't be a real holiday unless you could have dinner with your feet in the sand. Leave the promenade towards the south: the versatile *Waikiki* is an institution, it also offers breakfast *(from 9.30am)*. Morning larks and those hoping to set sail early (e.g. for the crossing to Lobos) should head to *La Luna* at the harbour *(C/ El Pulpo | €–€€)*. With its view of the lake, this restaurant is a good shout at all hours of the day.

Secreto del Sur (C/ Guirre | Oasis Tamarindo, Local 26) supplies delicious ice cream, as well as muesli, croissants, cakes and more. A central alternative for coffee and ice cream is *Il Gelato Puro (C/ Lepanto 2 | ilgelato puro.com)*, where you can sit inside or outside.

Corralejo is your best bet for vegetarian and vegan options, with several restaurants dedicated solely or predominantly to healthy, meat-free eating and others following suit, at least to some extent. *H2O (daily 9am–5pm | C/ La Milagrosa 29)* in the central square is a lovely vegan café that has adapted the usual fare of Spanish sandwiches *(bocadillos)*, salads and burgers.

LAND OF FREEDOM

This unusual tapas bar serves slow food and is excellent value for money. It pairs six different five-course menus with wines to perfectly complement each course. There is always a vegetarian and vegan menu to choose from, three of the menus can be made gluten-free and there are two children's meals. Of course, you can also go à la carte and choose from starters, main courses and pasta. The owner is Italian, the cuisine Italian-Canarian. *Evenings only, closed Tue | at the Hotel Lobos Bahia Club off the main road near C/ Gran Canaria | tel. 626 22 09 08 | landoffreedom.eu | €€€*

SIDER TIP
Five-course indulgence plus wine

MESÓN LAS TEJAS

The restaurant to visit if you're craving meat and fish! It fills up extremely quickly because of its great food. *Closed Wed | C/ Arístides Hernández Morán 2 | near Waikiki | tel. 676 31 01 94 | €*

PAST & FUTURE

The new alternative to *Sanus*. Landlady Aida moved here from Cologne, Germany, and her healthy and tasty menu has found plenty of takers – especially the very reasonable lunch menus *(Mon/Tue, Thu/Fri only)*. All ingredients are fresh and recipes draw on Mediterranean cuisine with the occasional Canarian touch. They even have a few tables outside. *Closed Wed, Sat/Sun evenings only | C/ Almirante Nelson | past-future.com | €*

SANUS

The trend for meat-free, healthy food was sorely missing on the island until recently. *Sanus* (Latin for "healthy") has gained such a good reputation that we recommend booking in advance. The restaurant offers delicious vegetarian, vegan and gluten-free meals with friendly service and atmosphere. Flexitarians are also welcome as the menu includes some excellent fish and meat options. *Evenings only, closed Sun | C/ Anzuelo 4 | tel. 928 53 65 85 | sanusfuerteventura.com | €€*

SHOPPING

You will find almost everything on the main road, but the prices are quite high. *Dany Sport (Av. Nuestra Señora del Carmen 42)*, the largest sports shop in the area, sells hiking and

Enjoy the sea breeze on a catamaran tour of the coast

camping equipment, swimming and sportswear and also roller skates.

Blanc du Nil (Av. Nuestra Señora del Carmen 37 | on the lower Water Park roundabout) sells men's and women's clothes made exclusively from white Egyptian cotton in a variety of cuts and weaves. In the dazzling heat of the summer, this cool white fabric is the perfect choice. *Little Paradise (C/ Lepanto 5)* specialises in surfing equipment. On Tuesdays and Fridays there is a – mainly African – *flea market (9am–1pm | on the main road near the Acua Water Park)* selling belts, cheap watches, jewellery, wood carvings, T-shirts and towels. There are also people who braid hair (don't forget to haggle!). Well worth visiting are the markets at the CC Campanario (10am–2pm): come on a Thursday for the arts and crafts or Saturday for the "green market", with fruit, vegetables, cheese, *mojo*, prickly-pear jam and much more. Sunday is the Canarian market where you'll find (almost) everything. This is an excellent place to browse, with jewellery, toys, textiles, ornaments and photos of the island all on offer. Particularly eye-catching are the pieces of black jewellery made from real island lava.

SPORT & ACTIVITIES

In the town itself, there are a mass of booths and shops which run from the harbour along the main road to CC Campanario, offering virtually every activity you can do in Corralejo and around, from buggy, jeep or quad tours to fishing trips and surfing lessons. Most of them are agencies offering the same tour with the same operator so the prices are the same wherever you choose to book. It may still be worth shopping around first though because not all agencies offer tours from the smaller operators, which can sometimes work out cheaper. The agency *Elerent (C/ Hernán Cortés 18, near Hotel Avanti)* is careful to choose its providers for quality and value for money.

A great choice for children is up on the roof of the *CC Plaza (C/ Carabela)* where the kids can play a round of mini-golf or let off steam on the trampoline.

ACUA WATER PARK

A fun day can be enjoyed by old and young alike: choose to slowly drift along the *Río Lento*, throw yourself down the Kamikaze slide or have a relaxing massage sitting under the waterfall in the wave pool. Many of the attractions appear twice: in a large version for the grown-ups and in miniature for the youngsters who particularly love this water park. *June–mid-Sept daily 10am–6pm; closed mid-Nov–end March; otherwise Fri–Tue 10.30am–5.30pm | admission 25 euros, seniors and children (under 12) 19 euros | acuawaterpark.com*

BICYCLES, SCOOTERS & E-SCOOTERS

In the town centre, bikes can be hired for a reasonable price from *Vulcano Biking (C/ Acorazado España 8 | tel. 928 53 57 06)* while the most extensive offers for mountain bikes, organised trips through the volcanic landscape and individually designed routes can be found at *Easy Riders (C/ Las Dunas | Local 2 | tel. 637 40 82 33 | easyriders-bikecenter.com)*, slightly hidden in the east of the town. Electric bikes are another fun alternative when the weather becomes too hot or windy. *Elerent (C/ Hernán Cortés 18 | tel. 604 14 86 49)* offer a particularly cheap rental service. They also hire out motorised scooters – recommended if you plan to cover longer distances.

INSIDER TIP
Cycle to a crater

NORTH OR SOUTH?

A SERIOUS DEBATE

"Don't you think the north is a lot nicer?" or "It's better here in the south, isn't it?" Those who have moved to the island to live and work are often so convinced that "their" part of the island is nicer; they rarely venture to other corners (except maybe to the airport or the capital) and they try and win guests (who have visited both) over to their side. To help you decide: the north has a more vibrant, urban and international feel; the south – including the Jandía Peninsula – is more geared towards package holiday tourism and is better for swimming. You may be left wondering about the island's interior ...

BOAT & FISHING TRIPS

Glide over the waves while being cooled by a gentle sea breeze and warmed by the sun – nothing could be more relaxing than a catamaran sailing cruise. The price includes pick-up from your hotel, a walk around the island of Lobos, and stops for swimming, snorkelling and eating on board. The leading tour operator sailing from the harbour is *Fuertecharter (tel. 928 34 47 34 | fuertecharter.com, with an excellent video)*, but the other operators can also be recommended. The best boats for fishing trips are catamaran barracudas such as *Barracuda Perdomo (tel. 630 35 53 91 | barracudafuerteventura.com)*. Information on all the boat and sailing trips is available from the white booths along the pier in Corralejo.

BUGGIES

Buggy tours are a popular albeit dusty way to explore the island. Guided tours on these two-seater, four-wheel vehicles are an exhilarating adventure; travelling virtually next to the ground, you head off road through the volcanic and dune landscape in the island's north. We recommend you try eco-buggies – all-electric, zero-noise and zero-emission speedsters which are permitted to drive through the dunes, meaning you discover more than on a traditional buggy. Child seats are also available *(booth in CC Campanario | tel. 647 28 83 39 | FB: twizzylanz)*. A more sophisticated, if less eco-friendly and more expensive alternative are the silver, three-wheel Canam-Spyder *(tel. 619 07 22 48 | canamfuerteventura.com)*. But remember you'll need a driving license for all these.

INSIDER TIP
Mountain fun, but make it eco

JET SKI

Ever wanted to race at high speeds over the waves? Then book a jet ski safari from the harbour quay on one of these "water motorbikes". *Booking: tel. 666 14 15 66 | jetskifuerteventura.com*

SCUBA DIVING & SNORKELLING

Dive down and explore the underwater world of El Río. This sheltered strait between Corralejo and Lobos attracts a great variety of fish making it ideal for snorkelling and scuba diving. Easy snorkelling safaris in the water off Lobos are available twice daily with *Get Wet (tel. 660 77 80 53, Udo | getwet-snorkelling-fuerteventura.com)*, also for children from five years of age.

To dive down to deeper levels, scuba-diving courses are offered at various points further along the coast. Ideal for beginners is Corralejos's oldest diving centre, *Dive Center Corralejo (C/ Nuestra Señora del Pino 22 | tel. 928 53 59 06 | divecentercorralejo.com)* which has its own learner diving pool. Miguel's team chooses diving spots along the north and east coast or at Lobos depending on the direction of wind and strength of waves. The diving base *Punta Amanay (C/ El Pulpo 5 | tel. 928 53 53 57 | puntaamanay.com)* is a similar establishment. Both centres are located near each other close to the harbour.

SEGWAYS

The alternative for all those who want to go faster than at walking pace: 2wheeltours *(CC Campanario | tel. 672 25 64 19 | 2wheeltourz.com)*

SURFING & PADDLEBOARDING

Windsurfing, kite surfing, surfing or stand-up paddling – the choice is yours in Corralejo. The most popular water sports centre for all kinds of water activities is *Flag Beach (tel. 928 86 63 89 | flagbeach.com)* based at the dune beach in the north between the resort and the Tres Islas Hotel. *Billabong (C/ La Red 11 | tel. 928 86 62 07 | billabongsurfcamp.com)* is another alternative within the resort itself offering surfing and SUP. Both offer inexpensive accommodation for tourists. If you want the one-to-one learning experience, you can take lessons from a former surfing world champion: *Marina Taylor Surf School (C/ La Gomera 5/Arena Beach | tel. 686 77 66 62 | marinataylorsurfschool.com).*

Sunwave (C/ Anzuelo 23 | tel. 928 86 73 07 | sunwavesurfcamp.de) specialises in surfing. As the domain suggests, course participants are also welcome to stay, either in a surfers' flat share or in a villa.

BEACHES

Playa de Corralejo does not refer to the small town beach, but the dune beach 5km further to the southeast at *Tres Islas* and *Oliva Beach* hotels. About 1.5km south of the hotels, where the traffic does not yet pass close to the beach, is a nudist area. Take note of the signal flags: if it is red, swimming is not allowed due to strong currents and if it is yellow you should stay close to the shore. The local beach by the small pier is popular with children, while the pebbled ground and shallow water of the beaches further south in the town's bay make them more suited to sunbathing than swimming.

NIGHTLIFE

★ Nightlife with a sea view. Nowhere on the island offers a more vibrant and buzzing atmosphere after sunset than

Riu Palace Tres Islas hotel pool

Corralejo. Evening entertainment consists of cocktails and live music in the town centre, along the promenade and in the bars on the pedestrianised zone (Calle Iglesia). Plaza Félix Estévez, otherwise known as "music square", is the main hub where musicians gather every evening to jam and everyone is invited to dance. The beats are louder at the bars and clubs clustered along the beach.

BUENA ONDA

The name gives it away: The "good wave" is the top surfer bar here and it gets crowded, especially late. And if you happen to have worked up an appetite, they also serve sandwiches, pizza and the like. *C/ la Niña 3 (off C/ Iglesia)*

GALERA BEACH CLUB

While this bar-restaurant with tapas opens early, it's at its best for a romantic sundowner enjoyed with your feet in the sand, as here you sit out on the beach. While the low sun makes your Aperol spritz sparkle, allow your gaze to wander over the town and the sea for a moment of pure bliss. *In the south of the bay at C/ Poseidon*

KACTUS

Kactus offers tapas and a whole range of cocktails, but it's the impressive gin and tonic menu that's the real draw. The menu boasts 27 varieties with staff more than happy to create extra combinations from the ingredients available. Sit back, relax and people-watch in one of the comfy chairs on the pedestrian zone or nab a seat on the roof terrace to enjoy the view. *C/ Iglesia 16*

SUNSET LOUNGE

Come in the evening to enjoy the beach-party vibes of this bar popular with, but not exclusively for, surfers. Crowds gather under the awning on the terrace with its windproof glass to quench their thirst with beer and cocktails. Louder sounds of hip-hop, house and funk are played at the weekend and there's live music on the podium. But caution: the bar closes at 10pm (earlier in winter) to respect the local residents. The guests then move on along the beach to the resort's centre. *Av. Grandes Playas 75/eastern end of Galera Beach*

Untainted island: Isla de los Lobos off the coast of Corralejo

WAIKIKI

An institution in Corralejo. Only here can you dream with sea views, your feet in the sand and a cool drink even at midnight. Plus there's dancing at the weekend. *C/ Aristides H. Morán*

AROUND CORRALEJO

1 CUEVA DEL LLANO

11.5km / 13 mins (by car) from Corralejo

A large sign on the main road points to this 648m-long lava cave; but if you follow the signs you could be disappointed, as the cave has been closed for some time because of the danger of falling rocks. However, you can look into the cave and also visit the small museum. *Wed/Thu 10am–3pm, Sat 3–6pm | admission free | 11km on the FV101 towards Villaverde, then follow the signposts "Cueva del Llano" to the right |* *G3*

2 ISLA DE LOS LOBOS ★

4km / 15 mins (by ferry) from Corralejo (harbour)

Take the ferry over to Isla de los Lobos to spend a few hours in a deserted wilderness. Those who spend their holiday in Corralejo should not miss out on an excursion to this small island named after "sea wolves", or monk seals. Because of its ecological diversity the site is a designated protected area. This virtually uninhabited car-free island has a walking trail, a beach, a tiny village and most of all unspoilt wilderness. You can learn

Still on the lookout for pirates: Torre del Tostón in Cotillo

more about the island's nature in the *Centro de Visitantes* at the jetty. The island's landscape is distinctly different from the main island; here no goats or other animals nibble away at the struggling vegetation, leaving this predominantly black lava rock greener and lusher than Fuerteventura. One advantage is that the beach is close to the quay (on the left) where visitors can relax and go scuba diving after visiting the island's lighthouse (8km there and back) or simply sunbathe in the bay. If you want to eat on the island, book a table in advance at Antonito in the village. You can also buy something to drink here or even better bring a large bottle of water and picnic with you from Corralejo. Remember to take your rubbish with you when you leave. And another thing, don't go looking for monk seals on the island – you won't find any. *Several daily crossings from 10am | H1–2*

3 LANZAROTE

13km / 25 mins by boat from Corralejo (harbour)

This island, which is well known for its natural wonders, can be seen from Corralejo. Boats travel between the islands several times daily, departing from the main pier. The crossing takes about 25 minutes with the normal ferry and about 12 minutes in the large catamaran. The travel agencies on the main road will have more information about guided day trips. *Detailed information can be found in the Marco Polo Lanzarote guide. 0*

COTILLO

(🕮 E3) **Too busy in Corralejo, too much going on at the shifting dune beach? Then head to Cotillo, a former fishing village with an authentic feel that looks much like Corralejo looked two or three decades ago. Although devoid of entertainment, the town is experiencing a growth in tourism.**

The main attractions are the beach and sea as well as restaurants along the pebble beach of the old port in the town centre. To protect the port, a defence tower, *Torre del Tostón*, was built in 1743 at the southern edge of the town; it is the only surviving historic building. (A sister tower, Caleta de Fuste, was built at the same time, see p. 78.) However, by that time the era of the dreaded pirate attacks was almost over, so the old walls do not have any dramatic tales to tell. Today it houses temporary art exhibitions. The nearby lime kilns are testimony to El Cotillo's former economic importance.

If you arrive by car the country road leads you straight into the town. Turn left just before the end of the town and you will reach the tower, the lime kilns, the new harbour, various restaurants and a large beach. Turn right just before the end and you will come to the centre around the old harbour. If you would like to go to the small swimming bays and to Punta de Tostón, just follow the main road that bends sharply to the right twice.

EATING & DRINKING

Seafood and fish lovers are in their element in Cotillo. Particularly noteworthy is *El Mirador (closed Thu | C/ Muelle de los Pescadores 19 | tel. 928 53 88 38 | €€)* at the old harbour, where you can enjoy the roof terrace with panoramic views. Even closer to the waves is *Vaca Azul (daily | northern side of the old harbour | tel. 928 53 86 85 | vacaazul.es | €€)*, which also has a terrace. The popular "Blue Cow" has long maintained a good standard with its typical Canarian fare. The friendly café-bar *La Ballena (C/ Pinito del Oro 1)* to the far south of town serves cakes, cocktails and tasty, freshly prepared meals for everyone arriving after a day's surfing or wanting to enjoy the view of the fortress and ocean. The best time to come is at sunset. The bakery-café *El Goloso (C/ León y Castillo | at the northern edge of town)* deserves special mention. The location is unspectacular, the interior little better, but the quality! And the taste! Think real wholemeal bread and good coffee but also probably the best *bocadillos* on the island, delicious French patisserie and fresh fruit juices and juice cocktails.

INSIDER TIP
Food worth travelling for

SHOPPING

Cotillo may not be a shopper's paradise, but that's all the more reason to take note of two very special shops. The first is *Lapa Studio (C/ 3 de Abril 13, towards the new harbour on the right |*

lapastudio.es) for "Art, Design, Décor": a small, fine design boutique which even has its own shoe brand. The second, *Islands Gourmet (Av. los Lagos, at Hotel Cotillo Beach)*, offers, as its name suggests, exquisite food for the pampered palate. The "Islands" referred to in the name are the Canary Islands. Alongside the usual Fuerte delicacies of goat's cheese, prickly-pear jam and *mojo* sauce, there is also palm honey from La Gomera and Lanzarote wine.

SPORT & ACTIVITIES

The beach south of Cotillo gets some large surf and attracts those who prefer waters that are a little more exciting, especially the bodyboarders and surfers. The *Star Surf School (Av. Los Lagos 42 | tel. 605 20 65 65 | starsurfschools.com)* on the way to the lagoon offers family discounts as well as yoga – and you can stay at the surf camp. *Riders Surf 'n Bike (C/ 3 de Abril 1979, #33 | tel. 629 25 88 61 | riders-surfnbike.com)*, along the main road, organises kite-surfing and stand-up paddling courses as well as bike rental.

Next to the windmill in the El Roque suburb, the riding stables *Granja Tara (tel. Fanny 607 55 26 61 | also transfer from Corralejo)* offer riding lessons and cross-country rides for experienced riders. Find an alternative means of transport at *Segway Tours (Av. Los Lagos/Hotel Cotillo Beach | tel. 630 98 42 81 | segway tours-fuerteventura.com)*.

BEACHES

The large beach below the fortress tower is not ideally suited to less confident swimmers or for surfing beginners, especially as the water hides shallow rocks in many places. The small bays north of the village, the *Playas de los Lagos*, are protected by reefs, meaning the water is always calm. Even children can swim there safely.

AROUND COTILLO

4 PUNTA DE TOSTÓN

4.5km / 7 mins (by car) from Cotillo

From Cotillo a cul-de-sac leads past the white sandy bathing bays of the

Playas de los Lagos to the northwestern cape 4km away, with lighthouses from three generations. The premises now house a *fishing museum (Tue–Sat 10.15am–5pm | admission 3 euros)*, which is dedicated to the traditional fishing methods of the *Majoreros* and there is also a small cafeteria. In the western foothills you can partake in the creation of land art: over the years visitors have built rock cairns from lava rocks some of which are now daring balancing acts of astounding heights. There is a track that takes you on to Corralejo via a dirt road (better not to attempt it in a normal car). During the summer months the area is full of Spanish campers. *E2*

5 LAJARES

8km / 8 mins (by car) from Cotillo

The island's most underrated resort also has an unusual history: originally a soulless farming community, the town has seen a transformation into a large surfer camp and Fuerteventura's mecca for arts and crafts. But let's go back to the beginning of the story for this hub of the alternative scene. It all started with the embroidery school and the sale of embroidered items at *Artesanía Lajares*. Embroidery is still practised at La Pirata on the main road, albeit on a far smaller scale and has been the inspiration for many tourists visiting the island. All the arts and crafts on display are made in the town and you can meet in person the creators of these beautiful items. A walk around this creative community starts on the road to Corralejo on your left-hand side: *Otro Mar* (decorative ceramics, *otro marceramics. com*), *Gusty Bags* (on your right; great canvas bags and

INSIDER TIP
Choose beautiful

Cairns compete with the lighthouses at Punta de Tostón

The beautifully renovated Casa de los Coroneles in Oliva

cushions, *gusty.eu*), *Vaca Loca* (on your left; fun felt plastics and jewellery made by Steffi), *Cabracadabra* (down on your right) with the silk painter *Lidia* (clothing, lamp fabrics, shoes) and the goldsmith *Bernhard Glauser (bernhardglauser.com)*, and next door the fashion designer Ulrike with her store *Ulitxu*; and finally surfer art at *North Shore*, which sells surfboards, including hand-painted, exclusive designs by Sonni Hönscheid – real showpieces!

North Shore is the town's oldest surf shop run by the German-born family Hönscheid – a name that's music to surfers' ears. Jürgen Hönscheid became Germany's first professional surfer at the beginning of the 1980s and his daughters followed in his footsteps. Sonni has also made a name for herself as an artist with her colourful surfboard designs (opposite the junction to Majanicho, *northshore-fuerteventura.com)*. Surfers are attracted to both the north and west coasts which is why the strategically positioned Lajares, despite its inland location, has become a popular place for surfers. The leading surf school is *Joyas Surf (tel. Jeff 616 08 45 09 | joyas-surf.com)*, whose boss is also an avid surfboard collector, so be sure to stop to talk shop! Along with a friend, he has designed his own T-shirts and drinking cups, and when it comes to surfing, nobody can fool him! Plus, he offers generous family deals and rates.

Popular meeting points for surfers are *Mana Café* and *Canela Café*, the latter also serves as a bar-restaurant offering more substantial meals. Live music is played at both venues usually on Wednesdays. An absolute must is the restaurant off the main road to Majanicho *(380m from the roundabout on the left)*: the *722° (Wed–Sun evenings, Sun also for lunch | tel. 928 94 70 05 | €€€)*. While you might worry the Canarian modernist architecture makes promises it can't keep, the fresh gourmet cuisine exceeds all expectations. This restaurant serves a small, changing menu with Italian/French/Canarian-inspired dishes, all in front of the most amazing sunset and a clear view out over the hills of Cotillo. There are also art exhibitions from time to time. *F3*

INSIDER TIP
Foie gras at dusk

LA OLIVA

(F4) **Certainly not a stunningly beautiful location, but La Oliva is a popular destination during the day for tourists based in Corralejo – and for everyone else it's a handy stopover on a trip around the island.**

La Oliva, the main resort in the island's north, still offers a few ancient walls and is the main destination for contemporary art in the Canary Islands. Opening hours in the town may vary, perhaps as a result of the lower visitor numbers, with the exception of the *Centro de Arte*.

SIGHTSEEING

CASA DE LA CILLA

This historic building was once an old church tithe barn used to store the farmers' levies. It now houses a museum dedicated to the islands crops and agricultural tools with information and displays of old photos that provide an insight into the hard lives of the farmers and the industry that formed the backbone of the island's economy. *Tue 10am–3pm and 4–6pm, Fri 10am–3pm, Sat 10am–2pm | admission 1.50 euros | on the road towards Cotillo on the left | 30 mins*

CASA DE LOS CORONELES

The two-storey residence with crenulated corner towers and 40 rooms is the most important secular building on the island. It was built in the 17th century as a manor. At the beginning of the 18th century, after the fall of the *señores*, the military government took occupation – hence its name which means "the colonels' house". In November 2006 the newly renovated building was reopened by King Juan Carlos. The interior has not been restored but part of the building is used for temporary art exhibitions. *Tue–Sun 10am–6pm | admission 3 euros | at the southern edge of town | 1 hr*

CENTRO DE ARTE – CASA MANÉ

The art centre, funded by a private foundation, is housed in the *Casa Mané* – a historic building – two underground exhibition halls and a large garden containing numerous sculptures. Most of the works on display are by local contemporary artists. *Mon–Fri 10am–5pm, Sat 10am–2pm | admission 4 euros | on the southern outskirts opposite the Casa de los Coroneles | 1 hr*

The sacred mountain of Tindaya is an imposing landmark west of La Oliva

IGLESIA DE NUESTRA SEÑORA DE LA CANDELARIA
The white triple-naved church was built in 1711. It features a decorative dark natural stone tower, a beautiful baroque altar of St Mary and a pulpit with effigies of the four evangelists. *No set opening times | village centre*

MUSEO LA FÁBRICA ALOE VERA
The focus here is on selling aloe vera products, although you can also see how the plants are cut open and the liquid is extracted. They grow on the field next to the museum. *Daily 10am–6pm | FV-101/direction Corralejo on the left-hand side*

SHOPPING

MERCADO DE LAS TRADICIONES
A small market selling fresh island products. It is held in a historical residential building, the *Casa del Coronel* (not to be confused with the large *Casa de los Coroneles*). *Tue and Fri 10am–2pm | C/ Tercio Don Juan de Austria*

AROUND LA OLIVA

6 TINDAYA
6km / 7 mins (by car) from La Oliva
After heading about 5km southwest on the main road from La Oliva you will come across *Montaña de Tindaya*

on your right-hand side. The almost 400-m-high volcano is made up of the marble-like volcanic rock (trachyte) and has the red colour of iron oxide. The ancient residents considered the mountain sacred and left more than 100 engravings of feet, although their significance is still not clear today. The mountain was declared a natural monument in 1994. Despite the fact that its historical importance was well known, in 1991 a mining company managed to obtain the rights to use it as a quarry. Although the work was later halted, the wound that has been ripped into the mountain is a testimony to political corruption which is so indifferent to the protection of nature and history and far more concerned with the amount of profit to be made. Hiking up the mountain is only possible with a previously obtained permit and a guide.

A little further along the road, on the slope of *Montaña Quemada* *(□ B–C5)* above a long wall you will see the monument to the poet, philosopher and Franco opponent, Miguel de Unamuno. He is the most famous Spanish author to write about Fuerteventura, although he did not come to the island of his own free will. His criticism of the Spanish government resulted in him being dismissed from his position at a university and sent into exile on Fuerteventura in 1924. *□ E–F4*

NEVER A DULL DAY – EVENTS ALL YEAR ROUND

The *Canary Islands International Music Festival* (Jan–early Feb) programmes concerts on Fuerteventura. At the *Fuerteventura en Música* (late June/early July, *festivalfem.com*), bands play at the lagoons north of El Cotillo – the atmosphere is great. In May at the mill in La Antigua, artisans present their crafts for a week at the *Feria Insular de Artesanía*. The highlight of the year is the *Windsurfing World Cup* in front of the lagoon of Playa Barca mid/end July – a two-week beach party *(Fuerteventura-worldcup.org)*. And during November people meet in Corralejo for the *International Kite Festival*.

7 VALLEBRÓN

9.5km / 12 mins (by car) from La Oliva

East of Tindaya, a winding uphill road leads to a viewing point, the *Mirador Montaña de la Muda*. There is a parking area with a pathway that takes you to the actual viewing platform with an explanatory panel (text in Spanish and English). From here you can view a large part of the northwest of the island, especially the holy Montaña de Tindaya. If you time your arrival for the early morning, just before sunrise, you will be able to see the intense red hues of the rocks.

Next the road heads east to the high valley *Vallebrón* with its little church and village, which has so far been mostly spared the impact of tourism. Here, more than anywhere else on the island, some of the traditional farming methods have remained in use. This is largely due to the fact that the area receives a little more rain than elsewhere. Carob and fig trees grow between the fields and the entire valley is a nature reserve. F-G5

PUERTO DEL ROSARIO

(G-H6) **Compared to the holiday resorts, the island's almost tourist-free capital is another world altogether. You might imagine you've taken a trip to the Spanish mainland.**

Sports boats and fishing boats bob about in the harbour at Puerto del Rosario

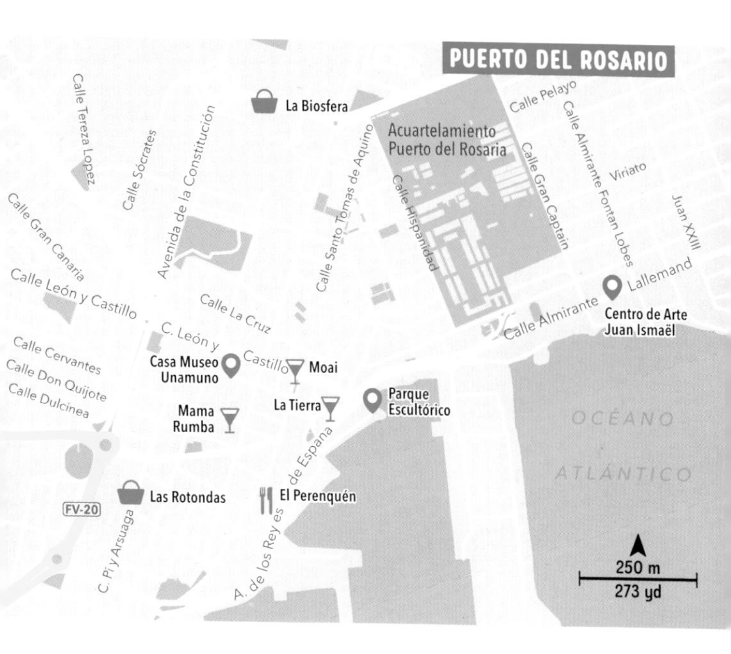

Puerto Rosario (the shorter form of the name) is neither very old nor is it especially beautiful, yet the harbour town with 28,000 inhabitants is the liveliest traditional town on the island.

From 1797 Puerto Rosario developed as the harbour for the nearby hamlet of Tetir, situated inland. A fresh spring attracted goats and so the new settlement was called *Puerto de Cabras* (Goat Harbour). In 1835 the little village had grown to 500 inhabitants and became a town in its own right, independent of Tetir. Its growth and development was then further increased by English merchants who shipped soda, dye (from the cochineal beetle) and lime from here in the 19th century.

Puerto de Cabras overtook the older towns as the most important port and as the central entrance to the island, and by 1860 was considered Fuerteventura's capital. From 1900, more and more administrative buildings went up and the first hotel opened its doors. Gradually the "goat harbour" name seemed inappropriate and in 1956 the town was renamed Puerto del Rosario (Port of the Rosary) in honour of the Our Lady of the Rosary, the town's patron saint.

Especially attractive is the town centre with the island's administrative seat *(Cabildo Insular)*, the church and the town hall. The improvements have also resulted in tourists from passing cruise ships visiting the town, much to the delight of its citizens and the town council. Puerto del Rosario also has the added attraction of its many cultural activities.

Here is one option for a local sightseeing tour: from the *Parque Municipal*, south of the bus station, where the two main roads cross, turn down the main road León y Castillo. The first building on your right is the wrestling arena. Behind the arena is the rectory. Head to the parallel road along the front of the house. Further down from here you will pass the *Casa Museo Unamuno* and the church will be on your left. At the next corner you will see the *Cabildo Insular* (the island's administrative building) on your right and on the left the town hall. Further down you will reach the harbour and its promenade. From here, go back up León y Castillo again and turn left at the town hall to reach the sizeable commercial centre which is also a pedestrian zone.

SIGHTSEEING

CASA MUSEO UNAMUNO

The museum is in the rooms of the former *Hotel Fuerteventura* where the Spanish writer and philosopher Miguel de Unamuno (1864–1936) lived for four months during his exile in 1924. Also staying with him was the journalist Rodrigo Soriano during his four-month exile in the same year. Visitors can take a trip into the past and view his writing desk, his bed and even his chamber pot and the kitchen, which have been kept exactly as they were during his day. *Mon–Fri 9am–2pm | admission free | next to the church | 30 mins.*

CENTRO DE ARTE JUAN ISMAËL

The three-storey building, with its yellow gabled façade, houses atmospheric exhibitions and event rooms as well as artists' studios. On display are contemporary artworks by Canary Island artists. *Tue–Sat 10am–1pm and 5–9pm | C/ Almirante Lallermand 30 | 40 mins.*

PARQUE ESCULTÓRICO

Some of the island's other open spaces have been embellished with sculptures and statues in recent years, but nowhere else are they as numerous or as interesting as the ones in the island's capital. There are more than 100, many with explanatory plaques. It all started with a sculptor symposium that was held here for ten years from 2001, and the best works remained in the town. Most of them adorn the promenade, but the *Parque Escultórico* (sculpture park) has no fixed boundaries and spreads all over the town. A free "Puerto on foot" route map distributed by the tourist information centre *(pavilion at the big roundabout opposite C/ León y Castillo | tel. 928 53 08 44 | turismopuertodelrosario.org)* will guide you to 16 of the town centre's art works.

EATING & DRINKING

The staff in nearly all the restaurants (and other venues) in Puerto del Rosario only understand Spanish. Of the cafés in the pedestrian precinct Avenida Primero de Mayo, you must try the Italian ice-cream parlour *Kiss (corner C/ Maestro de Falla)*, which also serves decent pizzas. Eating and drinking in an air-conditioned setting is possible on the upper floor of the shopping centre *Las Rotondas*.

EL PERENQUÉN

The perfect stop for a light meal or snack during your tour of the island's capital. On the terrace with a view over the port, the friendly staff serve up filled bread rolls and baguettes, light meals, drinks, coffee and cakes. *Mon–Fri 8am–4pm, Fri also 8pm until midnight | C/ García Escámez 5 | €*

SHOPPING

LA BIOSFERA

The weekly market on the top floor of the bus station was established especially to sell the island's produce – everything is very fresh and organic. *Sat 9am–2pm | Estación de Guaguas*

LAS ROTONDAS

Between the first and the second roundabout heading south is the town's very conspicuous shopping centre – a destination in itself. Around 100 stores are spread over four floors and there is also a large underground car park. Instead of escalators, pram-friendly rolling ramps link the floors. In addition to the usual clothing and sports gear, you will find children's clothing and toy shops, telephone shops and a supermarket. The restaurant level (top floor) also has a kindergarten and playground.

Gramophone in Museo Unamuno

NIGHTLIFE

If you are feeling adventurous, you should leave your resort for one Saturday night and explore the local nightlife. Nowhere on the island will you find such attractive and authentic bars and as much Latin dance fun as here (e.g. in *Mama Rumba*). Bars and clubs only open at about 11pm and smart casual clothing is preferred, that means no sandals, running shoes, baseball caps or T-shirts!

MAMA RUMBA

INSIDER TIP
Dance yourself happy!

Fancy taking to the floor with Spaniards or Latinos? Tourists are few and far between in the crowd here at Saturday's best night in the capital. *C/ San Roque 17 | close to Cabildo Insular*

Ancient handicraft: basket weaver in Ecomuseo La Alcogida in Tefia

MOAI
Puerto Rosario's trendy bar for after-sunset hours. Professionally prepared drinks served in a relaxed atmosphere with Latino pop sounds. It's the in-place for weekend nights in the island's capital. *Thu–Sat from 10pm | C/ León y Castillo 28*

LA TIERRA
Fed up with R&B and hip-hop? Then head to the town's most popular music club which offers a platform for all budding musicians. Located among the pubs along the harbour, this crowd-puller is open not just at weekends. Wednesdays is jam session. *C/ Eustaquio Gopar s/n*

AROUND PUERTO DEL ROSARIO

8 TETIR
9km / 10 mins (by car) from Puerto del Rosario

From Puerto del Rosario you drive on the old main road to Corralejo, past the island's former airport *Los Estancos*. The old landing strip crossed over the road which had to be closed every time an aeroplane took off or landed. The church village of Tetir, at one point the parish church of Puerto del Rosario, is the focal point of this fertile valley.

The terraced fields on the valley slopes – once used to grow cereals and prickly pears – are relics of an era when agriculture was still very important and provided the inhabitants with a degree of prosperity. Tetir's parish church (consecrated 1745), the *Iglesia de Santo Domingo de Guzmán* with its baroque altar, bears witness to this prosperity.

9 ECOMUSEO LA ALCOGIDA ★

20km /20 mins (by car) from Puerto del Rosario

The huge outdoor museum in Tefía takes you back to a not-so-very-distant rural world. A tour takes you round seven restored farms where the rooms are furnished as they as they used to be, as if the inhabitants had just popped out for a moment. Elsewhere there are domestic animals and they have also faithfully reproduced some workshops, although not all of them function every day. You can buy their products (including wickerwork, tin work and ceramics) and sometimes there is even freshly baked bread. The entrance building complete with cafeteria is by the car park west of the road through Tefía at the southern end of the village. *Tue–Sat 10am–6pm | admission 5 euros, children 2.50 euros | 1½ hrs | E6*

A GOOD NIGHT'S SLEEP

AWAY FROM THE TOURIST TRAFFIC!

Country hotel *Maroh (Sitio de Juan Bello | Villaverde, on the FV-101, on your right from Corralejo opposite Campesino | tel. 928 86 80 50 | mahoh.com | €€)* offers a romantic retreat behind walls of lava stone with garden and typical Canarian flora. All nine rooms are complete with chic bathroom and at night you'll sleep under a canopy. The hotel's rustic restaurant has a personal feel to it and serves Canarian cuisine with some clever twists.

SURFING COLORS APARTMENTS

Welcome to the *Surfing Colors apartments (C/ Pejin 2 | Corralejo | tel. 670 77 71 89 | surfingcolors.com | €–€€)*. The complex gets its name from the colourful frescoes and surfing waves painted on the walls of the 91 apartment rooms, all with self-catering kitchenette. The complex is situated within Corralejo town which makes it an unusual yet practical base for your holiday. There are two small pools and you can also book a surfing course.

THE CENTRE

PALM OASES, CHURCHES & FISHING VILLAGES

This will be your first encounter with Fuerteventura if you arrive by plane. The first impression is a sobering one: you will see little more than the grey-yellow monotony of the semi-industrial and commercial section of the town.

Tourists head straight out towards the north, or else south to the Jandía Peninsula. But at some point most return to the centre region as four of the island's five places of historic importance are here: Antigua, Betancuria, Pájara and Tuineje, which govern the

Betancuria

municipalities of the same names. The island's busiest tourist centre of Caleta de Fuste is close to the airport, while the bays of the coast heading south are lined with picturesque fishing villages and friendly Gran Tarajal.

The area is divided into a wide, trough-shaped extended valley with a mountainous area to the west – up to 722m – with deep valleys and beautiful palm oases. Some farming still takes place here, mainly for the cultivation of tomatoes and aloe vera.

THE CENTRE

Valle de Santa Inés
4 Tegú
Betancuria ★ p.72
Ziegenfarm 3
Antigu
p.7
25km, 35 mins
Ajuy (Puerto de la Peña) 1
5 Vega de Río de las Palmas
6 Barranco de las Peñitas ★
Valles de C
Toto
10
Tiscamanit
Mühlenmu
Pájara parish church ★
Pájara
p.70
2 Tuineje
37km, 35 mins
La Florida
Rosa de
Catalina García
Río Gran Tarajal
FV-2
Gran Tarajal 13
Oasis Park ★ 14
La Lajita
FV-2
Tarajalejo
p.84

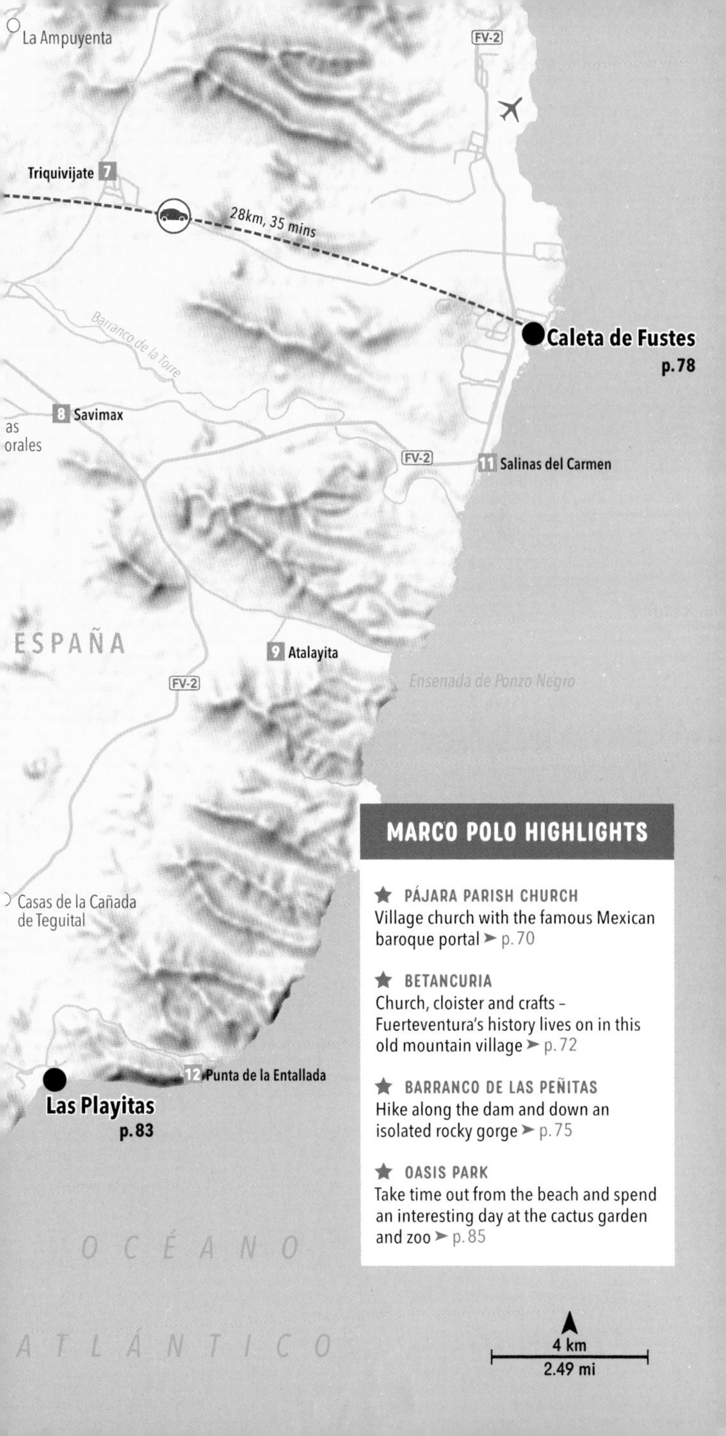

La Ampuyenta
FV-2
Triquivijate 7
28km, 35 mins
Barranco de la Torre
Caleta de Fustes
p. 78
8 Savimax
as
orales
FV-2
11 Salinas del Carmen
ESPAÑA
9 Atalayita
FV-2
Ensenada de Ponzo Negro
Casas de la Cañada
de Teguital
12 Punta de la Entallada
Las Playitas
p. 83
OCÉANO
ATLÁNTICO
4 km
2.49 mi
MARCO POLO HIGHLIGHTS
★ PÁJARA PARISH CHURCH
Village church with the famous Mexican baroque portal ➤ p. 70
★ BETANCURIA
Church, cloister and crafts – Fuerteventura's history lives on in this old mountain village ➤ p. 72
★ BARRANCO DE LAS PEÑITAS
Hike along the dam and down an isolated rocky gorge ➤ p. 75
★ OASIS PARK
Take time out from the beach and spend an interesting day at the cactus garden and zoo ➤ p. 85

Hiking trail with a sea view at Ajuy/Puerto de la Peña

PÁJARA

(🕮 C–D9) **The entire southwest of the island is administered by this well-kept village, where you can sense the prosperity that tourism has brought to the region.**

Examples of this are the modern town hall and the fact that the town has the first public swimming pool on the island. The small, terraced fields on the surrounding slopes still bear witness to the fact that this area was also once intensively cultivated. The most visible legacy from that period is the parish church. *Parking space in the barranco below the church and town hall | access from the road to Betancuria*

SIGHTSEEING

PÁJARA PARISH CHURCH ★

The nave of the *Iglesia de Nuestra Señora de Regla* was built between the 17th century and the beginning of the 18th century. The church became known for its beautiful Mexican baroque façade with Aztec elements. In addition to the geometric sun patterns it also has snakes, jaguars and birds. It was, for a long time, a mystery as to how the stone portal could have been transported all the way from Mexico to this remote village. Today, however, we know that the unknown stonemason must have copied the patterns from an Italian sample book and that neither the stone nor the portal façade came from Mexico. The dark interior of the church has a stunning Mudéjar-style wooden ceiling. The Mudéjar style developed during the 14th and 15th centuries in Spain as a combination of the Moorish and Gothic styles and was used for a long time on the island. The beautifully gilded baroque altars were completed in 1785. In the afternoons when the sun shines it seems as if they are lit up by spotlights – thanks to small windows that were built so high up that you cannot see them from the church's interior. Right at the entrance is a machine that turns on real spotlights for 1 euro. *Daily 10am–5pm, although it may close earlier | ⏲ 30 mins.*

EATING & DRINKING

CASA ISAÍTAS

Careful restoration work transformed this 200-year-old ruined manor house into a real gem. It's an intimate four-roomed guesthouse *(€€€)* with two beautiful inner courtyards and a good and atmospheric restaurant that is famous for its selection of delicious tapas. *Daily 11am–4pm | opposite the parking lot below the church | tel. 928 16 14 02 | casaisaitas.com | €€*

AROUND PÁJARA

1 AJUY (PUERTO DE LA PEÑA)

9km/5.6 mi / 10 mins (by car) from Pájara

This small fishing village with the two names is a popular sightseeing destination thanks to its location on a black-sand beach and to the nearby "pirate caves". Electricity and running water were only introduced in 1986 but the village no longer sees much fishing. Those in need of some sustenance should go to the "Golden Cage", the *Jaula de Oro (€€)*. Its prime location, directly on the beach, is reflected in its prices and service. A more affordable alternative is *Casa Pepin (€)* higher up on the slope but still with a lovely sea view from the terrace. On the same street (above the car park) is the *Trecepeces Shop* selling pretty arts and crafts as well as souvenirs.

At the north end of the beach a footpath leads like a ramp over an almost white rocky plateau to the *Caleta Negra* bay where enormous caves have been eroded by the sea. To get there, walk across the plateau to the north, past the old lime kilns (two small gorges below) and follow the signposts for "Caleta Negra" to the steep downhill steps. You find yourself in the larger of the two "pirate caves". The second cave is just next to it.

Continue an hour further on foot (4.5km there and back) for a sight that is even more special in the solitude the island is known for. This second destination is the impressive rock arch that rises at the mouth of the *Barranco de la Peña*, north of Ajuy, and delimits the sea like a real-life picture frame. You reach it by following the road that branches off above the lime kilns; continue above Caleta Negra, then go inland up to the next path running north to the *barranco*, then turn left. In front of the rock arch is a natural swimming pool, perfect for a cooling dip. *C8*

2 TUINEJE

9km / 12 mins (by car) from Pájara

The village Tuineje is the Cinderella among the old island communities. Well worth a look is the unusual altarpiece in the *San Miguel* parish church (late 18th century) depicting the glorious battle of Tamasite in which a heroic bunch of 37 farmers under the command of the island's captain managed to chase away a troupe of British buccaneers back in 1740. The key to the church can be obtained in the house opposite the west side of the church, the one that has a rather striking commemorative plaque for a pious nun. *9km southeast of Pájara | D–E9*

BETANCURIA

(D7) **No tour of the island is complete without a visit to this historic town. ★ Betancuria was founded in 1405 by the Norman Jean de Béthencourt, who had conquered the island in the name of the Castilian crown.**

The little village (700 inhabitants) can only be reached via winding mountain roads and is the smallest municipality on the island. It is very pretty with a number of restored old mansions. Life here is influenced by tourism today. Park at the southern entrance to the village, then walk to the church along the footpath.

SIGHTSEEING

CASA SANTA MARÍA

The island's most beautiful features are on display here, and not just in the main attraction, the amazing multimedia show and the 3D cinema with underwater footage *(last shows 3.15pm)*. Also very interesting are the historical photos and farming equipment as well as an embroidery demonstration; the "virtual goat shed" is a good laugh and be sure to linger in the peaceful shaded garden. *Mon–Sat 10am–3.30pm | admission 6 euros | entrance past the restaurant with the same name | casasantamaria.net | 1 hr*

INSIDER TIP
15 minutes of inspiration

CONVENTO DE SAN BUENAVENTURA

In the valley before the northern entrance of the town are the ruins of a 17th-century Franciscan monastery. Since the secularisation of the monastery in 1836, the citizens have used the site as a stone quarry which is why the cloister, for example, is gone. Opposite the church is a chapel that was built in front of a cave where, during the 15th century, San Diego (a miracle worker and missionary) was believed to have lived.

IGLESIA DE SANTA MARÍA

The current church that towers over the valley floor was built in 1620 to replace the first cathedral which was destroyed by pirates in 1593. The triple-naved church is built in the island's typical Mudéjar style (with wooden ceilings). There are several altars, including the beautiful baroque main altar that dates back to 1684. In the left niche of the altar on the southern wall (to the right of the entrance when seen from the inside) is a carved wooden statue of Santa Catalina. It is regarded as one of the oldest surviving works of art on the island. The sacristy *(entrance left of the altar room)* with its carved and painted wooden ceiling is also worth seeing. *Mon–Sat 10am–12.30pm, 1–3.50pm, Sun 10.30am–2.20pm | admission 1.50 euros |* ⏲ *45 mins*

MUSEO ARQUEOLÓGICO

The museum is on the main road but is currently undergoing major renovation work with no date set for its reopening. The collection centres around the history of the island's indigenous population and their culture. *On the main road*

EATING & DRINKING

For a snack, go to the *Casa Santa María cafeteria (Plaza Santa María 1 | access from below | €)*, which serves drinks and home-made cake in a separate part of the garden. Just as green and shady are the garden restaurants *Taberna* and *La Sombra* where you can enjoy tapas and well-reviewed burgers. *Don Carmelo (between Casa Sana María and the road)* pleases his guests with tapas in a typically Canarian setting.

CASA SANTA MARÍA

This award-winning restaurant is stylish and romantic without being over-the-top. Particularly the two inner courtyards are a sheer delight. The kitchen serves sophisticated Canarian dishes. *Mon–Sat 10am–5pm, hot food served from 12pm, closed from the end of May for 4 weeks | at the church square | tel. 928 87 82 82 | casasantamaria.net | €€€*

SHOPPING

In various shops below the Casa Santa María you will find the island's best and most varied range of arts and crafts on sale. The items are from all over the island and include culinary delights such as prickly-pear jam and jars of ready-made *mojo* sauce.

Culinary courtyards at Casa Santa María

The goal of every hike through the Barranco de las Peñitas is the Ermita de la Peña

AROUND BETANCURIA

3 FINCA PEPE

2km / 4 mins (by car) from Betancuria

Goats, goats and more goats at tjis goat farm. From the *Finca Pepe* car park walk through the middle of the goat barn – and a lot of bleating – to the cheese dairy, where you can watch the goat's milk being processed and cheese being made. Unsurprisingly, there's also a range of fresh goat's cheese and other goat's milk products for sale. *From FV 30 opposite the monastery ruins 1.6km up the hill | D7*

4 TEGÚ

3.5km / 7 mins (by car) from Betancuria

From the top of the pass at the Tegú mountain (645m) north of the town you will get a lovely view of the island's old capital, Betancuria, and of the vast northern part of the island. The viewing point and car park is dominated by two large statues, which represent the ancient Fuerteventura kings (or chiefs) Guise and Ayose – heroic images of rather dubious artistic value. The *Mirador Morro Velosa (Tue–Sat 10am–6pm)*, higher up at 640m, offers even more impressive panoramic views of the landscape as well as a small museum and a café. *D7*

5 VEGA DE RÍO DE LAS PALMAS

5km / 6 mins (by car) from Betancuria

Probably the island's most beautiful palm tree oasis, this farming settlement is also called *Vega de Río Palma*. The 17th-century *village church* on the left-hand side *(daily 10.30am–1pm, 4–6pm)* has the largest shrine on the island: a 23-cm alabaster figurine of the *Virgen de la Peña*. This figure of Mary is thought to be the oldest on the island and was probably brought here from France during the 15th century by the conqueror Jean de Béthencourt. As patron saint of the island, every September the virgin is the destination of the largest pilgrimage on the island. At the church square, the fine delicatessen and restaurant *Don Antonio (closed evenings and Tue | tel. 928 87 87 57 | restaurantedonantonio.net | €€-€€€)* is a great place to recharge your batteries. The restaurant has earned its excellent reputation and is sure to delight more senses than just the taste buds with its wonderfully leafy, tranquil inner courtyard. ▯ D8

IDER TIP
it in an oasis
in an oasis

6 BARRANCO DE LAS PEÑITAS ★

6.5km/10 mins (by car) from Betancuria

From the southern end of the oasis you can go on one of the most beautiful hikes that the island has to offer to the rocky *Barranco de las Peñitas*. Drive 400m towards Pájara and, as the main road starts to climb, take a right turn into the valley at Vega de Río Palma (signposted) and go a further 1,300m to where the road crosses the creek for a second time and park your car. From there you can walk down the valley along the dry riverbed towards the reservoir. After 15 minutes, just before the tamarisk forest, leave the riverbed to the right (just after another distinctive track that also turns right) and continue above the forest and then along the silted-up *Embalse de las Peñitas* reservoir. After 10–15 minutes you will reach the dam. Just beyond it the path leads down through two bends to the dramatic rocky gorge. After a few minutes you will reach the whitewashed *Ermita de la Peña* chapel, a cool, peaceful place of rest and quiet contemplation. When the wind blows through the rocks here it makes some rather eerie sounds, like the whispers of a ghostly choir! To return you need to backtrack on the same path. The whole hike should take about 90 minutes (including a bit of a break). At some places you will need to be very surefooted and don't forget to take drinking water! Back at the starting point of the hike, visit the heavenly *Casa de la Naturaleza (Mon–Sat 10am–5pm | €€)*, a place to cheer both body and soul. It has an exhibition on the animal and plant world (excellent photos and multimedia show), a cafeteria and tapas bar and a beautiful, paradisiacal Canarian atmosphere. Enjoy indoors or outdoors in the shade of the palm trees. ▯ C–D8

ANTIGUA

(▯ E7–8) **Arriving from the north, you are welcomed to La Antigua by the historical windmill that houses the cheese museum.**

The town is surrounded by a wide valley that has been settled since the late 15th century when Andalusian and Norman settlers arrived and began to cultivate the valley's red, fertile soil. Today La Antigua administers the surrounding community (with the same name), which includes the holiday resort of Caleta de Fuste.

SIGHTSEEING

IGLESIA DE NUESTRA SEÑORA

The white parish church – dedicated to the Virgin of Antigua – dominates the centre of the community. The large building has a single nave and bell tower and was completed in 1785. Don't miss the Mudéjar ceiling in the choir and the ochre-coloured classical altar. Palm trees and plants offer shade in the tastefully renovated square. *Daily 9am–1pm | ⏲ 20 mins.*

MUSEO DEL QUESO MAJORERO

You love goat's cheese? At the cheese museum you can learn about the history of traditional cheese-making and about the goats themselves who provide the raw materials. Exhibition room 1, however, first informs visitors about the Canary Islands' geological origins. The spacious gardens surrounding the estate are beautiful to see as is the cactus garden under palm groves at the back. The museum also houses a cafeteria with a small shop selling different cheeses as well as handicrafts.

Many regular visitors to Fuerteventura probably know the museum better as the old "Molino de Antigua". In fact this small, beautifully renovated mill is still one of the island's most important landmarks and it can be visited by tourists. *Tue–Sat 10am–6pm, Nov–April until 5.30pm | admission 4 euros | on the FV 20 north of the town | ⏲ 1 hr.*

EATING & DRINKING

TODO BUENO

You have to be confident of your abilities if you name your restaurant "All Good". But, holding true to its name, this restaurant serves delicious Italian dishes such as goat meat bolognese. The owner, Francesco, is inspired by the island's traditional cuisine. Treat yourself to one of their exquisite desserts. *Daily | on the FV 416 diagonally opposite the church | tel. 928 87 87 56 | €–€€*

AROUND ANTIGUA

7 TRIQUIVIJATE

5km /5 mins (by car) from Antigua

This little hamlet east of Antigua would not be worth the visit if it was not for the fine restaurant *Antonia (Piedra Blanca 146 | tel. 644 14 71 57 | antoniatriquivijate.com | €€€).* It opens only if you pre-book at least 48 hours in advance. Master chef Kira Schilling will tell you the daily specialities on the phone. What she whips up depends on the season, because she refuses to use anything but the best. Monday to Friday there is a fixed lunch menu, but the dinner *(daily)* menu varies. You dine in a lovely courtyard or an elegant living room. You can't get

Say cheese! Museo del Queso Majorero in Antigua

more individual than that! Another local destination is the *Crines del Viento stables (at the northern exit to the village | tel. 678 21 31 08)*, which offers horse-riding excursions, including for beginners, and is happy to pick guests up from Caleta de Fuste. *F7*

8 SAVIMAX

6.5km / 10 mins (by car) from Antigua

On the Savimax aloe vera plantation you can see this age-old medicinal plant up close. Also on sale at the factory are the products that are derived from it. *At the roundabout on the FV 50 go 5km in the direction of Valles de Ortega and, after 150m, turn left onto the estate | E8*

9 ATALAYITA

17km / 16 mins (by car) from Antigua

If you fancy a quick visit to the stone age, then turn off the FV 2 on to the dead-end road to Pozo Negro and, after about 3km, you will see a road that turns right on to a new track. It runs diagonally across the black lava flow that continues to the coast and leads to the most important ruins of structures built by the island's original pre-Hispanic inhabitants: Atalayita (F9). Excavations have uncovered various small and inconspicuous igloo-like huts made from lava rock, many of which have been restored. It seems to have been a shepherd settlement and the shelters were probably not used as homes but for storage and drying meat. From the 15th century, larger, rectangular buildings were added, including some shelters for livestock. The solidified lava flow (outflow of the Malpaís Grande lava field) where the goats of the indigenous Canary Island inhabitants roamed, was created by one of the island's last eruptions about ten thousand years ago. On the summit of the hill to the east of the hut settlement you can look out over the whole terrain.

The fishing village, *Pozo Negro* (📖 *G9*) consists of little more than two rows of houses on a bay with a black pebble and dark sand beach. Two lovely bar/restaurants with sea views serve fresh fish *(€)*.

10 TISCAMANITA/MILL MUSEUM

8.5km / 15 mins (by car) from Antigua
Everything you always wanted to know about mills... In Tiscamanita you can visit the well-designed mill museum *(Centro de Interpretación de los Molinos)*, which is housed in a restored windmill with adjoining farm buildings. It has a well-preserved collection that provides insights into Fuerteventura's traditional milling trade and its history. Every guest receives a complimentary sample of *gofio. Tue–Sat 10am–6pm; Nov–April 9.30am–5.30pm | admission 4 euros | coming from Antigua, turn right uphill at the left turn when you enter the village | no museum parking | 📖 E9*

CALETA DE FUSTE

(📖 *G8*) **The holiday resort Caleta de Fuste was developed in the 1980s on a gently curved south-facing bay on the island's east coast, just 7km south of the airport.**

It is very popular with British holidaymakers. In brochures, maps and on signs it is also referred to as Costa Caleta, Playa de Castillo, Castillo de Fuste or El Castillo. The "Castillo" refers to the *Castillo de Fuste*, a round stone tower that was built in 1740 as the town's defence against pirates. Today it forms a decorative part of the hotel complex, *Barceló Castillo Beach Resort*.

EATING & DRINKING

Nothing on the island compares to the stylish gastronomy on the harbour,

Fishing boats in tranquil Pozo Negro on the east coast

characterised by its contemporary, elegant ambience and white décor as well as excellent sea views throughout. Up in the harbour building (with terrace) you can eat in the buffet restaurant *La Ancla (evenings only | €€€)*, while the ground floor houses the à la carte restaurant *El Camarote (€€)* for a romantic sunset dinner on the terrace, the ice-cream parlour *La Goleta* and the bar *Noray*. At the front of the pier, the lounge bar *El Faro (daily 10am–1am)* with its panoramic view completes the excellent choice on offer here. You can eat inside or outside at any one of the bars or restaurants *(tel. for all: 928 16 31 00)*. *La Perlita* to the northeast of the beach, the Beach Café at the hotel *Geranios* (both providing snacks only) both offer views out to sea. At the south end of the bay, the pleasant beach bar *La Isla (€€)* also serves meals and, situated on a man-made island, can only be reached via a bridge. *El Capitán (opposite the Barceló Fuerteventura | tel. 928 16 3723 | €–€€)* is a very popular tapas bar with Canarian atmosphere, a palm tree terrace and live music. Alternatively, you'll get a lot of bang for your buck at *Café Gala (downstairs in CC Atlántico)*, a great choice for breakfast.

ASCENSIÓN

A well-hidden little gem, this eatery offers friendly service and a rather unusual selection of meat, including ostrich and kangaroo! Don't worry, vegetarians are safe here too – try the incredible mushroom and walnut risotto. Plus, it's all freshly prepared. *Daily, evenings only | in the Puerta del Sol apartment complex, C/ Alcalde Marcial Sánchez Velázquez | tel. 654 28 43 79 | €€*

LA FRASQUITA

"Fresh fish only" reads the sign, and yes, the only restaurant right on the beach here also stands out because the landlord has a share in a fishing boat. The special of the day is shown to you "in person" before being served up with *papas arrugadas* (wrinkly potatoes) and a small salad. The *mojo verde* is probably the best on the island. *Closed Wed | western side of the beach | tel. 928 94 12 77 | €€*

VOLCANO

The heading "A fuego lento" (slow-cooked) on this eatery's menu reveals that the emphasis here is on quality – something you might notice in the waiting times, too. After all, everything is freshly prepared. All of it? Well, alright, you don't have to wait the 72 hours it takes for the Galician veal to cook in the oven. *Closed Mon | CC El Castillo, Local 6–7 (car park side) | tel. 928 54 76 45 | volcanorestaurant.es | €€–€€€*

INSIDER TIP
Lovingly cooked

SHOPPING

Shopping centres are dotted all over the island; the largest of them is *CC Atlántico* in the south offering the widest selection of goods (clothing, sport items, food and electronic goods), all shops being fully air-conditioned. Most shoppers come here for the bargain prices at the large supermarket *Eurospar Padilla*. Tuesday and Saturday are market days *(9am–2pm | in the west close to the road)* where you can pick up wood carvings, clothing, jewellery and much more besides.

SPORT & ACTIVITIES

From the town you can either head up into the mountains or down into the sea depending on your chosen activity. Explore the island's interior and coastline on two, three or four wheels or else go scuba-diving; both should be high on your list of priorities if you're of the adventurous type. Fun and excitement can be had for young and old alike in the basement of the CC Atlántico: the *Mega Park Family Entertainment Center* is a big draw with bowling, snooker and slot machines. Next door is a cinema. This is the ideal spot for bad weather, especially as there is no shortage of restaurants and cafés. Children will be happiest on the beach-side forecourt, where trampolines, climbing frames and other challenges await. Children will also enjoy a variety of spots within the town, e.g. trampolining and a bouncy castle on the central street, a playground at *CC El Castillo* and a second one 400m further towards the harbour. There is also a mini-golf course on the beach side of the *Barceló Hotel Fuerteventura* (access from the promenade), and another tucked away by the harbour, 150m along the promenade on the rocky shore.

BIKES, BUGGIES & TRIKES

More than anywhere else, the island's rugged volcanic landscape is on your doorstep waiting to be explored. How you choose to explore your surroundings is entirely up to you. Originally from England, affable Geoff owns *Caleta Cycles (at the beachside Hotel Geranios | tel. 676 60 01 90)* and takes guests on guided bike tours. He also has a wide selection of rental bikes. *Quad & Buggy Adventure & Safari (tel. 928 86 65 52 | quadadventure.net)* organises buggy safaris, including a visit to a goat dairy. Motorbikes and bicycles are available to hire from *East Coast Rides (tel. 693 24 92 45 | eastcoastrides.es)*. It's best to avoid the popular e-scooters because they're only allowed on expanded cycle paths and there aren't any in built-up areas (and most areas around here are built up!). However, the real hit, especially for couples, are the organised trike tours. There's just something about being blown along by the wind on a rolling sofa, or you can have a go at steering for yourself. The only operator is *Cool Runnings (CC El Castillo | on the car park side | tel. 649 93 85 81 | fuertetrikes.com)*.

INSIDER TIP
Couchsurfing with a difference

BOAT TOURS

Oceanarium in the harbour offers a range of activities from dolphin- and whale-watching boat trips, semi-submarine tours to explore the underwater world and deep-sea fishing (see below). The large catamaran *Oby Cat (tel. 636 59 55 81 | obycat.com)* is also anchored at the harbour waiting to take passengers to the bay of Pozo Negro for a spot of snorkelling followed by a steaming paella to be enjoyed on board.

GOLF

South of the town there are two 18-hole golf courses next to each other: the *Fuerteventura Golf Club (tel. 928 16 00 34 | fuerteventuragolfclub.com)* and the *Golf Club Salinas de Antigua (tel. 928 87 72 72 | salinasgolf.com)*. The former is also the older and larger of the two with long stretches, but both are par 70 and have views of the Atlantic.

OCEANARIUM

A popular destination for everyone, offering boat trips (see above) as well as kayak and peddle-boat hire, jet skiing, jet packing or flyboarding and even swimming with sea lions. Children have a great time playing on the inflatable water play area. *In the harbour area | tel. 928 54 76 87 | oceanariumexplorer.com*

WATER SPORTS

Let's start with diving: the diving school *Deep Blue (tel. 928 16 37 12 | deepblue-diving.com)* has an ideal location at the harbour. Volker and his team know the best diving spots to be reached by boat from their own jetty. They take you to see fantastic underwater lava formations where you can spot shoals of brightly coloured fish hiding in the crevices and caves.

The resort would not be complete without a surfing centre, and *Canary Surf Academy (tel. 647 93 06 08)* is at the beachside Hotel Geranios. The bay is particularly suitable for beginners (and for paddle boarding). There are no windsurfing courses right now, but that may well change, so do enquire.

Why wait? Windsurfing boards lined up on the beach at Caleta de Fuste

Las Playitas

BEACHES

This shallow bay without any significant surf is perfect for less-confident swimmers, although the beach itself is not perfect. Most of the sand is not natural and is heavily compacted and interspersed with pebbles. On the east side, however, there is a special area for beach volleyball. Head further south to beach bar *La Isla* for better natural sand. There are also fun little pedal boats there shaped like convertibles and swans!

WELLNESS

Why not treat yourself to some real pampering? Non-guests are also welcome at the *Thalasso Spa (western side of the beach | tel. 928 16 09 61)* to take advantage of the great range of massages and treatments from head to toe, whether that be detox, manicure, aromatherapy or more. You can also relax in either the indoor or outdoor pool. A reduced price of 15 euros applies after 5pm (otherwise it's 25 euros).

NIGHTLIFE

A show or live music can be enjoyed every evening at *Piero's (CC El Castillo | pieroscafe.com)*, an old favourite. The *Beach Café (until 11pm | Hotel Geranios | at the westerly point of the beach)* shakes up cocktails with a sea view. Unsurpassed are the bars directly on the harbour where *El Faro* doesn't close until after midnight. Don't miss happy hour, which is widely offered in Caleta. The *Millennium Bar (CC Castillo Centro, UG)* does 2-4-1 on beer and wine until 10pm, while over in *El Capitán (opposite the Barceló Fuerteventura)* happy hour is from 7.30 to 9.30pm with beer, wine and sangría at amazing prices.

AROUND CALETA DE FUSTE

11 SALINAS DEL CARMEN

4km / 15 mins by bike from Caleta de Fuste

South of Caleta de Fuste you turn left to the *Salinas del Carmen* salt pans and the *Salt Museum (daily 10am–6pm | admission 6 euros)*. The road leads directly up to the entrance and the cleverly designed visitor centre with interactive media, which you should visit first before walking through the salt pans. For demonstration purposes the salt pans are still operated in the traditional manner, non-commercially of course. There's also a brand-new café-restaurant. As well as the sea salt harvested here, the museum shop sells other island specialities, including *gofio* biscuits. *G8–9*

LAS PLAYITAS

(E11) **The name Las Playitas, "The Little Beaches", refers to the peaceful fishing village at the end of the road.**

The larger of the "little" beaches is separated from the village by a small hill and has been developed into a holiday destination mainly for families and sports enthusiasts. In the picturesque old village with its whitewashed cubist houses, visitors and locals alike are attracted by the modest promenade and the small pier.

EATING & DRINKING

LA RAMPA DE TÍO ENRIQUE

Freshly caught fish with a sea view! At "Uncle Henry's" you can choose from the freshly caught fish which the waiter shows to you at your table. *Closed Mon, closed Sun evenings | Av. Miramar 1 (at the pier) | tel. 928 34 40 04 | €€*

SPORT & ACTIVITIES

The *Playitas Grand Resort* is a huge sports resort geared towards both amateurs and professionals and it has an Olympic-sized swimming pool fit for competitions. Other facilities include tennis courts, beach volleyball, the *Cycle Centre* with bicycle hire and organised bicycle tours, the scuba-diving school *Deep Blue (tel. 653 51 26 38 | deep-blue-diving.com)* and the surf and sailing school *Wellenkind (tel. 673 04 88 50 | wellenkind-surfschool.com)* which also offers windsurfing and SUP (courses and equipment rental).

The showpiece of the ambitious sports resort is its 18-hole golf course. They also offer golf lessons for beginners and advanced players (complete courses or individual lessons) *(access on the east side near the Playitas Hotel | bookings at playitas.net)*. The different sports providers here don't belong to the hotel and non-hotel guests are also very welcome.

BEACHES

The beach is a good 300m long and has black sand. Like all beaches in Spain, it is public, as is the access through the hotel grounds (or alternatively you can reach it from the village). You can rent umbrellas and there are showers and a nice beach bar.

Prickly yet picturesque: the cactus garden in Oasis Park

AROUND LAS PLAYITAS

12 PUNTA DE LA ENTALLADA

7km / 10 mins (by car) from Las Playitas

At Las Playitas an asphalt road turns off to the east. It leads uphill to the southeastern cape *Punta de la Entallada*, which has a picturesque lighthouse on its highest point. *F11*

13 GRAN TARAJAL

6.5km / 8 mins (by car) from Las Playitas

There is nothing particularly special about this sleepy little port town (pop. 10,000) but, if you have been here once, you might be among those who keep returning. Gran Tarajal, which has yet to see mass tourism, has a pretty beach promenade with plenty of restaurants. It is also known for its street art as it boasts 32 murals, some of which are several storeys high and impressively witty and imaginative. The best are around Calle Tindaya/Hierro and Calle Amanay/Vigan. For a bite to eat – with a panoramic view of the beach – try *Pizza & Pomodoro (€)*, the best place on the promenade. *E11*

TARAJALEJO

(C12) **On a long, black-pebble beach on the southern coast, the simple holiday complex Tarajalejo was developed next to a small, simple fishing village.**

With just one holiday complex in the entire place, this is a relaxing, low-key resort boasting a 1km stretch of beach which you might have all to yourself. A sun umbrella plus two loungers costs "just" 9 euros per day here – considerably less than elsewhere on the island.

EATING & DRINKING

At the town end of the beach, in Calle Isidro Díaz, two restaurants have beautiful terraces with sea views. *La Barraca (closed Tue | tel. 928 16 10 89 | €)* serves reasonably priced fresh fish, while *Adeyu (daily | tel. 928 16 10 85 | €)* specialises in pizza. You won't find their "Pizza Tarajalejo" anywhere else on the island: topped with dates, figs and goat's cheese, it's beguilingly fruity and sweet!

INSIDER TIP **One for the curious – figs on pizza?**

SPORT & ACTIVITIES

Autos Rent (C/ La Marisma | tel. 928 54 71 53) arranges quad tours and tours with the lowered "buggies" (for those who need it...). A branch of the *Ocean World (C/ Isidro Díaz 14E | tel. 928 87 54 44 | oceanworld.com)* diving schools completes the rather modest range of activities on offer.

AROUND TARAJELEJO

14 OASIS PARK ★

5km / 5 mins (by car) from Tarajalejo

This has evolved into one of the main attractions on the island – after the beaches. Here you can enjoy yourself all day long, and if you come back a year later you will be amazed to see what has been added. The nucleus, the zoo, is a spacious shady park with tall trees and flowering shrubs. The main attractions are the very funny parrot show *(last performance 12.15pm)* and three open-air theatres, one each for reptiles, birds of prey and brilliantly trained seals. A new attraction is the opportunity for an up-close meeting with lemurs – great for children. The zoo continues westwards into a palm and cactus garden complete with bird of prey theatre. The somewhat inappropriately named *Ecotour* sees a free open-top bus connect the more distant points on the edges of the park. Route 2 leaves the park proper and travels across the nearby hills for an incredible panoramic view of park and sea (heading towards the elephants, be sure to sit on the right for the best view).

The zoo includes three garden bars, a plant shop and a home and garden supplies shop. Don't miss the popular camel safaris up to a viewpoint on a dune. On Sundays *(9am–1.30pm)* the *Mercado Agro-Artesanal* – the largest market for island products from cabbages to ceramics, soaps to sauces – takes place in the grounds in front of the zoo entrance proper. It's colourful and well worth a visit. *Park open daily 9am–6pm | admission 38 euros, children (4–11) 19.50 euros | on the FV 2 near La Lajita (free buses twice daily from all holiday resort towns) | fuerteventuraoasispark.com | 5–6 hrs | C12*

INSIDER TIP **Island treasures**

THE SOUTH

SWIMMING FUN & ISOLATED OPEN SPACES

This is the picture book part of Fuerteventura – nothing but sun, sand and sea. On the 20-km stretch of Playas de Sotavento you can enjoy sea views from (almost) all the hotel room windows. Out on the waves, the sails of the windsurfers add bright splashes of colour. The beaches are never crowded and the surf is gentle.

German visitors established the first holiday accommodation in Morro Jable. Shortly after that, in 1970, the Robinson Club was set

Beach on the Jandía Peninsula

up in one of the first hotels. The name was very apt because the Jandía Peninsula was almost entirely deserted back then.

The long, sandy and wonderfully isolated beaches of Playas de Sotavento are only half the story – the Jandía Peninsula stretches beyond the southern cape at Morro Jable for another 17km to the west, and on the other side is the elongated, remote northwest coast.

Between the two coasts is mountain country and *Pico de Jandía*, the island's highest, cloud-covered peak at 807m.

THE SOUTH

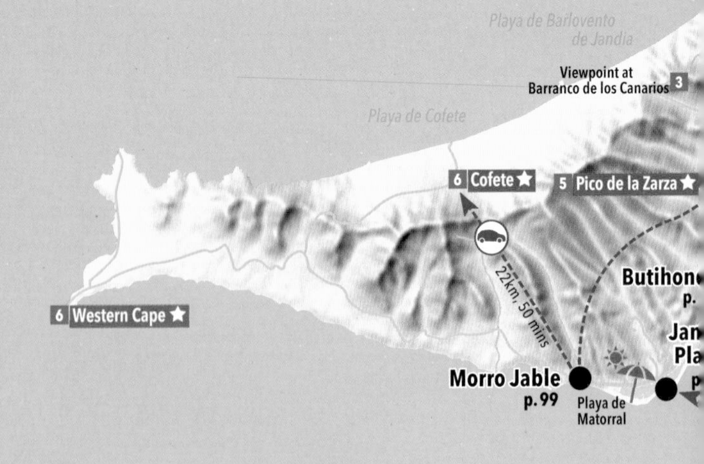
OCÉANO
ATLÁNTICO
Playa de Barlovento de Jandia
Viewpoint at Barranco de los Canarios 3
Playa de Cofete
6 Cofete
5 Pico de la Zarza
22km, 50 mins
6 Western Cape
Morro Jable p.99
Playa de Matorral

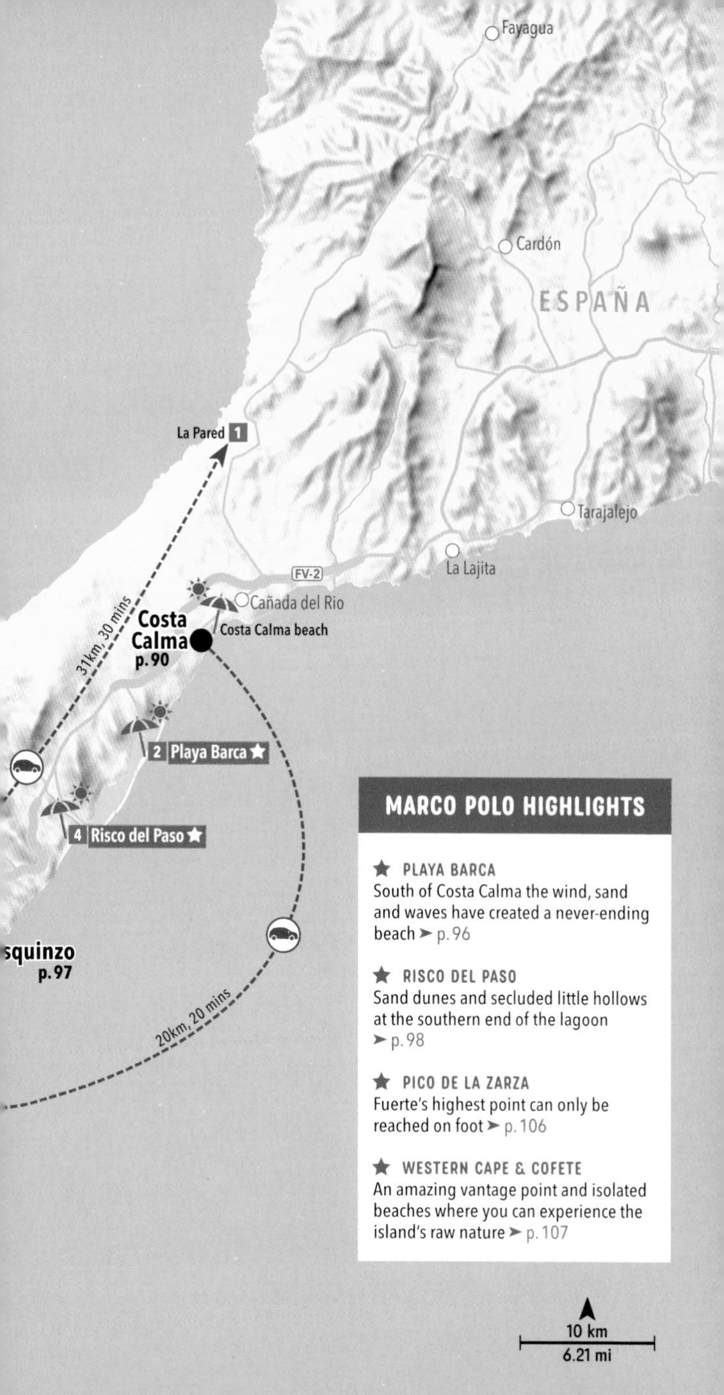

Fayagua
Cardón
ESPAÑA
La Pared 1
31km, 30 mins
Tarajalejo
La Lajita
FV-2
Cañada del Rio
Costa Calma p. 90
Costa Calma beach
2 Playa Barca ★
4 Risco del Paso ★
squinzo p. 97
20km, 20 mins
MARCO POLO HIGHLIGHTS
★ PLAYA BARCA
South of Costa Calma the wind, sand and waves have created a never-ending beach ➤ p. 96
★ RISCO DEL PASO
Sand dunes and secluded little hollows at the southern end of the lagoon ➤ p. 98
★ PICO DE LA ZARZA
Fuerte's highest point can only be reached on foot ➤ p. 106
★ WESTERN CAPE & COFETE
An amazing vantage point and isolated beaches where you can experience the island's raw nature ➤ p. 107
10 km
6.21 mi

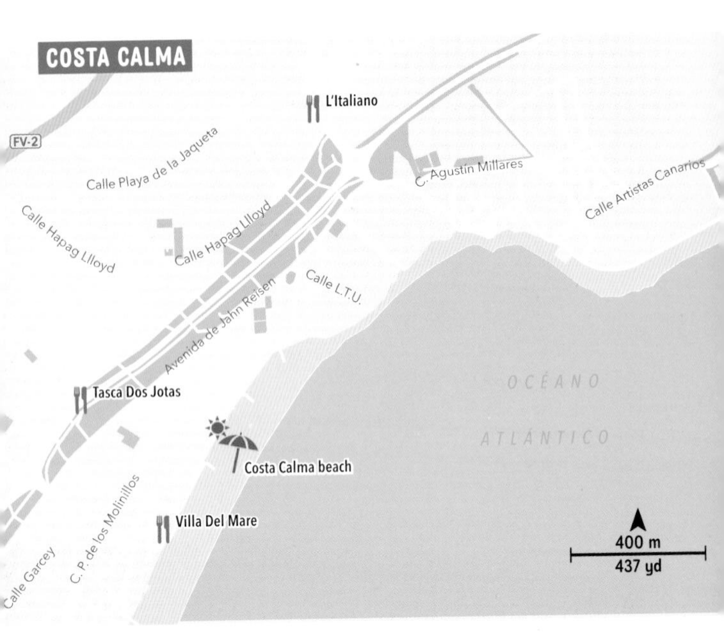

COSTA CALMA

(◫ B12) **Costa Calma, the "calm coast", refers to the holiday zone on the Istmo de la Pared at the start of the Jandía Peninsula.**

The area that lies furthest east is also known as Cañada del Río. The flat terrain on both sides of the main road has allowed – and still allows – building and over the years many bungalow and apartment complexes have sprung up. In between them are also some larger hotels but they are relatively unobtrusive (visually) and the rather unexpectedly lush green forest alongside the country road is what makes the biggest impression.

Costa Calma is spread out and there is no real village centre or appealing townscape. Between the scattered holiday zones there are sections of fallow land. Yet, as a guest, you will not want for anything. After all, what more could you need than the sun, a sandy beach and clear water?

EATING & DRINKING

The food scene is largely concentrated in several small shopping and eating complexes: *Centros Comerciales Costa Calma* and *Bahía Calma* in the centre, *Sotavento* in the east and *Internacional, Plaza* and *Palmeral* at the top end of the old road near the petrol station. A traditional favourite *Fuerte Action* is housed on the ground floor of *CC Palmeral* where you can hang out all day from breakfast until nightcap, tasting your way through their selection of juices, coffees, cocktails and snacks. Practically in the same complex, just one floor above *(CC Plaza)*, is *Kapé*, the place for coffee aficionados: the coffee beans are freshly roasted and the cake and snacks are also extremely tasty.

Two local mainstays are the Italian restaurants in *CC Costa Calma*: the slightly less expensive *Mamma Mia (€)* and the more upmarket *Arena (€–€€)*. If your budget is feeling the strain, *Mamma Mia* offers a three-course meal for €9.99 before 6pm. From there, cross the road and on the south side of *CC Bahía Calma* is *Rapa Nui*, a popular surfers' café serving breakfast, tapas, nachos, baguettes, cake and cocktails from morning until night. The best *chiringuitos* – beach bar – is definitely *Aurelia* thanks to regular live music sessions and a wind-sheltered children's play area. Ice cream is available at the German-owned *Eisdealer*, 100m along the main road from CC Bahía Calma. Sit out on the terrace until sundown.

Lots of sand and sun: the beach at Costa Calma

L'ITALIANO

For excellent pasta and pizzas like the ones they make in *Napoli*, including a selection of white pizzas (no tomato sauce). If you choose the (admittedly delicious) focaccia as a starter, one is enough to share! *Closed Mon | Plaza Hapag-Lloyd, in CC Cañada del Rio on the right | tel. 928 87 53 71 | €*

TASCA DOS JOTAS

This cosy Spanish/Canarian restaurant with white linen tablecloths makes a refreshing change from the town's run-of-the-mill pizzerias, snack bars and surfer bars. The establishment's speciality is goat and goat kid. *Closed Sun–Mon | CC Palmeral, upper floor | tel. 928 87 51 06 | €€–€€€*

VILLA DEL MARE

The new star on the local restaurant scene, complete with terrace and sea view! This restaurant serves up Italian dishes with a Canarian and international twist that are good enough to impress any gourmet. The setting is

Explore the sandy paths of the Costa Calma by mountain bike

INSIDER TIP
Two halves – twice the enjoyment

elegant and crisply whitewashed. A good tip is that many dishes can be ordered in half portions if you want to squeeze in multiple courses! The perfect place to celebrate a special occasion or to end your holiday in style. *Daily | below CC Bahía Calma | tel. 928 17 09 34 | villa-delmare.com* | €€€ | *XO*

SHOPPING

There are seven mostly small shopping centres spread through the holiday zone. The largest supermarket is in the new *CC Bahía Calma* while the shops in the *CC Sotavento (opposite the Hotel Taro Beach)* stock the largest range of watches, jewellery, cosmetics and sunglasses. The *CC El Palmeral*, close to the petrol station, is the most interesting, with shops like *Freestyle* (sportswear, including second-hand surfboards), or the surf shop *Fuerte Action*, and the great jewellery shop *1. Stone*.

In the *Boutique Tangente (in the hotel Costa Calma Palace, 1 floor below reception)* Bea Stein, who has been living on the island for years, sells original, ready-to-wear clothing collections, including larger sizes. Ask about her fashion shows – an island novelty. Bea asks her customers if they have time and would like to take part (your chance to shine?). All ages and physiques welcome!

INSIDER TIP
Model for a day?

The mainly African market that travels around the island in weekly cycles comes to Costa Calma on Wednesdays and Sundays *(9am–2pm | at the lower large roundabout)*.

SPORT & ACTIVITIES

BICYCLE & MOTORBIKE

Volcano Bike (tel. 639 73 87 43, Ralph | volcano-bike.com) will deliver a mountain bike to your hotel for you; they also offer guided tours from easy to sweaty. Off-road dirt-bike tours are organised by *Sahara Sports (tel. 669 79 71 62, Frank | enduro-guru.com)*. *Xtreme (at the Hotel Taro Beach | tel. 928 87 56 30 | xtreme-car-rental.com)* offers quad, trike and buggy tours, hires out bicycles and motorbike and can connect sailing, fishing and jet-ski trips. Whether with motor or muscle power, do not miss out on the guided tours.

JET SKI & WATERSKI

All kinds of water sports, including peddle boats, banana boats (and "hot dogs", suitable for children), kayaks, jet skis and waterskis are on offer at a well-managed station to the north of the beach at the hotel *Barlovento (tel. 616 43 71 84 | excursionesmarytierra.com)*.

SCUBA DIVING

Simona and Kay run *Fuerte Divers* in the Hotel Costa Calma Beach *(penultimate hotel before the northern edge of the beach | entrance through the hotel garden | tel. 628 01 77 17 | fuertedivers.com)*. Not only the nicest diving instructors imaginable, the couple make their dives more exciting with sunken wrecks and by creating their own underwater biotopes made from specially designed frames to entice diverse sea life. Divers are transported to the diving spots in powerful, motorised dinghies.

SURFING

The best way to try your hand at riding the waves is to be picked up from your hotel by one of the operators based in La Pared – for example *Waveguru* or *Wellenkind* (see La Pared p. 95) – as the only suitable waves can be found on the west coast of Fuerteventura. In Costa Calma, contact *Rapa Nui (CC Bahía Calma | tel. 928 54 91 40 | rapanui-surfschool.com)*, the surf school with the café/bar of the same name. It also has a fine surf camp.

TOURS

Prickly pears are a delicious fruit yet a nightmare to peel if you don't have the knack. Learn how to master the art by taking one of Kristina's excellent tours in the island's south: Her *Tapas Tour* takes you to an olive plantation and a cheese dairy. Or visit one of the island's wineries to taste Fuerteventura wine accompanied with snacks on the *Volcano and Wine Tour* led by a vintner. *Wild coasts & Legends* takes you to the rugged west coast, and then there's goat trekking – hiking with a real-life goat friend! It's important to book well in advance because Kristina can only accommodate small groups. *Tel. 617 69 40 67 | fuerte-authentic-tours.com*

INSIDER TIP **Nice to bleat you**

WINDSURFING

The epitome of the Fuerteventura feeling! Wind- and kite-surfers from around the world flock to the paradise setting of Playa Barca *(▯ B12)* for the strong gusts of wind which sweep through the mountains, for its expansive lagoon in tune with the rhythm of the tides and for its landscape dominated exclusively by sand, sea and skies. The first to discover the region's potential was René Egli in 1984 when he opened his own surf station here (today: *René Egli by Meliá*). It soon became the largest on the island and known worldwide for the surfers' world cup held here regularly in July. René Egli's *kitesurf station (tel. 928 54 74 83 | rene-egli.com)* lies directly below *Hotel Meliá Gorriones*; the windsurfing centre is approx. 200m away in the direction of Costa Calma. Guests can also be picked up from Morro Jable or Costa Calma.

If you prefer quieter, low-key alternatives and shorter distances, then surf with *Ion Club (tel. 661 34 96 89 | ionclubfuerte.com)* at Costa Calma beach (between *Costa Calma Palace* and *Monica Beach Hotel*). The kitesurfing station in Risco del Paso also belongs to the club – a fantastic location at the south end of the large lagoon. The centre provides transport.

BEACHES

Boasting 1.8km of soft yellow sand, Costa Calma's beach is split into two sections and there's plenty of room to play ball and run about. Two loungers plus parasol comes in at 12 euros per day. There are also two beach bars: *Horizonte* and *Aureola*. The latter, in particular, is worth a visit with frequent live music and, more importantly, a children's playground that's located so that you can keep an eye on what the kids are up to from your table. *Aureola* is south of *Bahía Calma, Horizonte* north at the *Monica Beach Resort*.

NIGHTLIFE

Dancing, drinking, chilling out – there's no better place for doing that than on the upper level of the *CC Bahía Calma* where you'll find no less than three prominent cocktail bars and clubs: *Los Piratas* (sounds like an outmoded place with pirate decorations, but this is far from true), *B-Side* (where things really get going from midnight onwards) and the *DVN*. This club/bar (its name is an abbreviation of *Divino*) has billiards and shishas on offer and is no less likable than its equally "divine" predecessor which had to be torn down.

Then there's the *San Borondón* at the *CC Sotavento*. Because of the hams hanging from the ceiling, you might at first suspect a folkloristic tourist trap. Fittingly, Félix, the proprietor, sometimes sings and plays guitar. But maybe you should wait until his son Ari stops waiting tables and starts singing *Hey Jude* or another Beatles classic on stage. On Saturday nights, he even performs with his band, which thrills the audience with emotional soul and intoxicating rock.

INSIDER TIP
Rhythm & Blues live

Kitesurfers make the most of the wind at Playa de Sotavento

AROUND COSTA CALMA

1 LA PARED

7.5km / 8 mins (by car) from Costa Calma

The narrowest part of the island, the desert-like *Istmo de la Pared* (Isthmus of the Wall) is situated near Costa Calma. One theory is that the wall separated two ancient Canarian kingdoms but there is no evidence to support this. The settlement of La Pared on the west coast has been named after the wall, and it is a place for visitors who either want to stay away from any hustle and bustle, or else they want to surf. For the west coast is ideal for surfing – especially at *El Viejo Rey* beach. The oldest of the three surf experts is *Waveguru (tel. 619 80 44 47 | waveguru.de/en/surfschool-index.html)*. Course participants can stay here for free at a surfcamp close to the beach.

Wellenkind (tel. 673 04 88 50 | wellenkind-surfschool.com), a surf school at hotel *La Pared*, is similar, again with its own camp. This is also a favourite with golfers, including those who want to learn how to play! The *Academia de Golf (tel. 616 24 94 59)* has a short, six-hole course and is the ideal place to learn as Irish professional golfer Ken Ellis gives the lessons.

On the other side of the *barranco* (at the first roundabout on the right), a cul-de-sac leads to a beautiful beach: small pools are formed by the tide in the shallow sedimentary rocks, little fish swim in the shallows at low tide, sea worms make strange patterns in

Explore the isolated terrain on a pony trek from La Pared

the sand and the ochre-coloured cliffs, black pebbles and reddish sand form changing patterns and contrasts. A footpath leads up to a rocky outcrop with a section that has been worn by the action of the waves into an arch. During high tide, and if the sea is rough, the seawater surges up and jets through the opening. While you're here you can grab a bite to eat at the car park. The Canarian restaurant *Bahía La Pared (tel. 928 54 90 30 | €€)* is a good option. There is also a reasonably sized swimming pool for guests and their children.

The stables *Rancho Barranco de los Caballos (tel. 619 27 53 89 | reitenfuerte.de)* offers experienced riders wonderful rides through the beautiful and isolated terrain on the wild western coast. Drive 20.5km on then left on the FV 605 in the direction of Pájara.

INSIDER TIP
The island's Wild West

Coming from Costa Calma on the country road, do not turn left towards the town, but take a right and follow the dirt road for 1.4km to *Quesería La Pastora (Mon–Fri 9am–6.30pm, Sat 9am–2pm)* where you can buy spicy goat's cheese directly from the producers. *B11*

2 PLAYA BARCA ★

5km / 5 mins (by car) from Costa Calma to Meliá Gorriones

South of Costa Calma is the most beautiful part of the Playas de Sotavento. Here, behind a narrow 4km-long spit of land barely 20m wide, is a large lagoon up to 500m wide that is dry at low tide or at least easy to wade through. The spit is

sometimes flooded, so be careful that your belongings don't float away! The only large building here is the *Meliá Gorriones* hotel. The Playa Barca is one of the best windsurfing spots in the world and every year in July the world championships take place here. *(◫ A13/B12)*

ESQUINZO / BUTIHONDO

(◫ D3) **From the motorway the Butihondo exit leads to two separate holiday resorts. In the part closer to the exit, you can turn left to the Robinson Club or right to several other large hotel complexes.**

But if you follow the "Farmacia" sign at the roundabout, the route takes you via the old road to the older part of *Esquinzo*. Parts of this area are very steep so quite a few of the hotel rooms have sea views. As the road runs above the resort, the area is also very quiet – and even the surrounding area quite peaceful. Buses travel to Morro Jable/Jandía Playa up to twice an hour from the main country road.

EATING & DRINKING

CASANOVA

The *Sensimar Royal Palm* hotel sells itself as an exclusive, fine-dining establishment. The spacious table setting and first-class service underline its exclusivity although the atmosphere is a little austere. The Italian-inspired cuisine is creative without losing sight of tradition. Treat yourself to at least two courses followed by a dessert. But if you enjoy a leisurely dinner, the five-course menu is also highly recommended. *Sensimar Royal Palm/last hotel in Butihondo in the direction Morro Jable | tel. 828 12 01 50 | €€€*

MARABÚ

Those who work in the tourism industry in the south, take their guests to this establishment. Everything here is spot on: the atmosphere, the service, the variety and quality of the food, as well as the value for money. Traditional island dishes, international dishes, fresh ingredients and good wine. There is also a terrace nicely sheltered from the wind. *Closed Sun | C/ Fuente de Hija | straight down from the country road | tel. 928 54 40 98 | e-marabu.com | €€€*

SPORT & ACTIVITIES

The water sports centre at the *Robinson Club (tel. 674 32 80 29 | ionclub fuerte.com)* has the widest choice of activities, including catamaran sailing, windsurfing and SUP. For tennis *(on artificial grass or clay courts)* and for swimming lessons visit *Matchpoint Sports (in the garden of the Fuerteventura Princess | tel. 928 54 4307 | matchpoint-world.de).* The latest craze is mermaid swimming where both legs are squeezed inside a fabric tail fin – swimming becomes no easy feat!

BEACHES

The long *Playa de Esquinzo* stretches out below the resorts. Good meeting points are the beach bars *Atalaya (below the Robinson Club)* and *Caretta Beach*. Note that nudism is the norm here. You can ignore any reservation signs on the lava-stone beach walls; the beach is public and reservations don't hold weight here.

NIGHTLIFE

The *Caretta Beach* bar *(closed Mon)* located below the *Club Jandía Princess* is a popular venue with good food and cocktails that only closes at midnight. Wednesdays *(from 8pm)* and Sundays *(from 1pm)* are for live music. In the old part of Esquinzo, the meeting place is *Safari Bar* at the *Monte del Mar* swimming pool.

AROUND ESQUINZO/ BUTIHONDO

3 VIEWPOINT AT BARRANCO DE LOS CANARIOS

10.5km / 15 mins (by car) from the Butihondo exit

Drive towards Costa Calma and take the old road at Mal Nombre and head down into the valley at the petrol station. After about 6km, where the road comes to an end, the panoramic landscape suddenly opens out in front of you. The desolate northern coast stretches westward until it reaches Punta Pesebre 15.6km. Cofete can also be spotted on the slope. However, the mysterious Villa Winter is hidden behind a ridge in the terrain. *D2*

INSIDER TIP **Understanding solitude**

4 RISCO DEL PASO ★

7km / 10 mins (by car) from the Butihondo exit

At Risco del Paso (turn off the country road on to an asphalt road) the Playa Barca lagoon ends. The attractions of this little stretch of beach – one of the most beautiful on the island – are its two small sand dunes with a long stretch of beach in between, and the grassy knolls with secluded little hollows protected from the wind.

Nudism is quite normal here. The sea in front of Risco del Paso is a favourite surf spot. (A13

MORRO JABLE/JANDÍA PLAYA

(C-D3) The double village of Morro Jable and Jandía Playa at the southernmost tip of Fuerteventura forms the largest tourist centre in the south. It consists of two very different sections.

Even though it's not very old, Morro Jable (or Morro del Jable) is a traditional harbour village in a beautiful location. East of it, on the other side of a hill, is now almost completely built up: hotels and apartment complexes make up the 3-km-long string of large holiday resorts that have come to be known as Jandía Playa or Jandía. The official names are *Solana de Matorral* or *Solana de Jandía*. Its beach is the *Playa de Matorral*.

Jandía Playa essentially consists of a leafy, elegant main road parallel to the coast with terraced hotel and apartment complexes built down the slope on one side. With its numerous bars, restaurants and shops it has become a lively promenade linking the hotel *Labranda World* (the former *Stella Canaris*) in the east with the old, clunky *Cosmo* shopping centre in the west. The promenade is particularly busy at night. A protected salt marsh stretches along the other side of the road; behind it lies the beach.

Show of flowers along the harbour promenade at Morro Jable

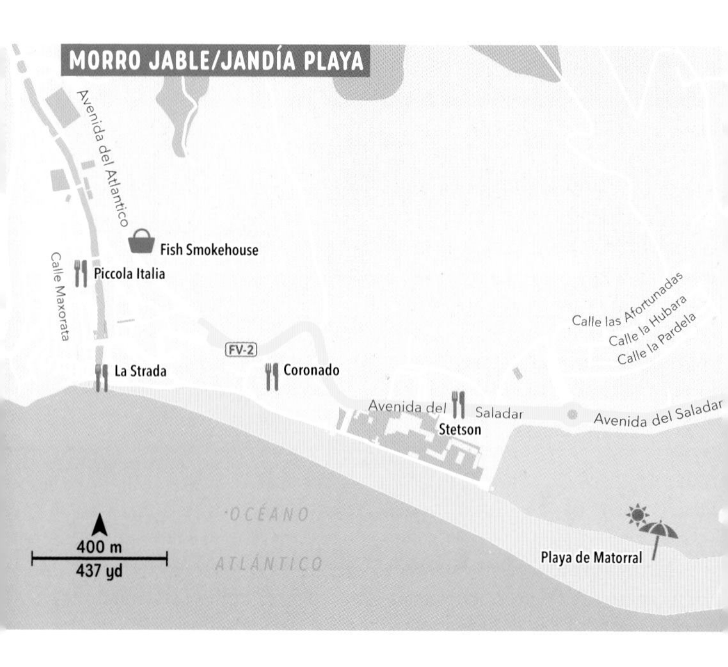

The beach promenade which starts at the Robinson Club and leads up to Morro Jable and the popular fish restaurants is smaller, quieter, more atmospheric and nearer the water. The simplicity and authentic Spanish nature of the old part of Morro Jable offers an interesting contrast to the artificial, large-scale holiday resorts in its immediate neighbourhood.

SIGHTSEEING

In the sea turtle conservation station at the harbour, you can watch the turtles swimming in the pool *(Mon–Fri 10am–1pm | to the right in front of the harbour gate)*. At the restaurant run by the fishing cooperative *(Cofradía)*, swarms of fish can be seen in the basin and with a bit of luck, you may catch a glimpse of rays skimming through the water.

EATING & DRINKING

You can have a lovely intimate lunch (or dinner) in Morro Jable. You will be able to dine better there on the beach promenade than at the restaurants on the main road at Jandía Playa. The restaurants all offer a very similar menus and the quality, food and price are much of a muchness. Recommended is the solid *Saavedra Clavijo (daily | tel. 928 16 60 80 | €€)*. If you prefer to eat well and don't mind missing out on the sea view, try the restaurants in the second row behind the promenade, where the food is better and/or cheaper, e.g. at *Charly (Plaza Cirilo López 1 | tel. 928 54 10 66*

| €€), a friendly local for many Spaniards and Germans who live there. The bars and restaurants situated in Morro's two narrow main streets in the pedestrian zone are not geared to tourists.

Among the many cafés and ice-cream parlours, the three worth mentioning are: the popular *California (Av. Saladar/at the taxi stand Casa Atlántica)* for ice cream, crêpes, juices, cocktails; *Eisdealer (30m further west)*; and *Magdalena (Av. Saladar 22d | on the hill near the petrol station)*, the coffee shop selling ice cream.

CORONADO

This is upmarket cuisine, and the menu features delicious combinations that blend Canarian, Mediterranean and Asian influences. Most of the ingredients are sourced locally from the island – and you can certainly taste the freshness. The prices are reasonable and the portions are good generous. The *Coronado* also offers beautiful accommodation. *Tue–Sat, evenings only | next to the Riu Palace Jandía | tel. 928 54 11 74 | restaurantecoronado.com | €€–€€€*

LA STRADA

This eatery just off the promenade has changed hands several times. Anyone who's eaten here recently is surely hoping the current owner will stay, because the Mediterranean/Canarian/international cuisine (with a tapas menu) is as fine as the excellent service and there are beautiful tables inside and out. *Evenings only (lunch service also in winter), closed Tue | C/*

Sea views are on the menu in Morro Jable

San Juan 14 | WhatsApp 605 53 44 93 (to book) | €€

PICCOLA ITALIA

This restaurant, "Little Italy", has its own classic stone oven and serves the most delicious wood-fired pizzas in town. *Daily | C/ del Carmen 39 | tel. 928 54 12 58 | €*

STETSON

This popular restaurant is all about the food: delicious steaks and other meat dishes, but also good fish, and wonderful creations for starters and desserts, everything lovingly prepared. The interior is alright too. *Only Tue–Sun evenings | CC Cosmo, upper floor | tel. 626 14 09 58 | gourmet-stetson.com | €€€*

SHOPPING

The main road has a good selection of diverse shops, including plenty of upmarket brand-name clothing, and there are some bargains to be had in Morro Jable. Approaching from Jandía you will reach the large supermarket *Padilla* in Morro Jable on the right of the street going to the valley (before the turning to the left). Thursday is market day on the main road at the open space next to CC Cosmo.

FISH SMOKEHOUSE

Something new. Sven and Udo prepare melt-in-your-mouth smoked fish. Sample it on mini rolls that can be eaten on the spot – delicious! *C/ Mascona 32/in the Mercado Municipal (inside on the far left)*

SPORT & ACTIVITIES

Morro boasts a wide range of activities on land and water. A round of mini-golf is always a good idea for the kids *(at Hotel Faro behind the shops)*. Another good option at low tide is a beach walk to Butihondo or Esquinzo *(from CC Ventura approx. 90 mins)*.

ACTIVITIES IN THE HARBOUR

Don't miss the chance to experience Fuerte from the ocean! Many activities are available at *Excursiones Mar y Tierra (tel. 616 43 71 84 | excursionesmarytierra.com)* whose station is on a pontoon in the harbour: jet ski, banana boats, speed boats, waterskis, wakeboarding and deep-sea fishing. The almost two-hour long jet-ski ride to the western cape is popular.

Aquasports (tel. 693 92 16 09 | aquasportsfuerteventura.com) offers similar activities but you can also take to the skies with a paraglider. For sport fishing you can go out on the *Yellowfin (tel. 676 26 34 39)*. Sailing excursions are fun and the catamarans are especially spacious. *Magic* and other

Catamarans moored at the beach in Morro Jable await adventurous sailors

catamarans are moored in the harbour and can be booked with the tour guide at the hotel.

If you prefer a more active pastime, why not set sail on the *Maxi*, a traditional monohull yacht. When the wind causes the boat to heel, or lean on its side, even the laziest sun worshipper will get an adrenalin kick. The *Maxi* is not always harboured in the port because it undertakes longer sailing trips *(tel. 683 32 62 18 | maxisailing.es)*.

The two-mast *Pedra Sartaña*, built in 1940, takes to the sea on Tuesdays to Saturdays at 9.15am and 2pm (in the winter 10.30am only) for the popular pirate tours *(tel. 670 74 51 91 | excursiones-barco-fuerteventura.com)*, which are great fun, especially for kids.

Take a first-row seat on the *Odyssee 3*, a glass-bottom catamaran, to watch an underwater cinematic show. But that's not all: the boat will stop along the way for you to swim, dive or even snorkel in the turquoise waters; there is even a slide into the water *(tel. 616 43 71 84)*. All the harbour operators provide transfer from/to your hotel.

Join a buggy tour to explore the deserted interior

BICYCLES

Volcano Bikes (station at the Club Aldiana | tel. 639 73 87 43 | volcano-bike.com) hires out bicycles and organises tours of varying lengths. Four-wheel pedal bikes also can be rented at the wooden shed *Tourist Info Centre* at the western end of the salt marsh.

GOLF

Tucked away in a side valley is the 18-hole *Jandía Golf (par 72 | Barranco de Vinamar | tel. 928 87 19 79 | jandia golf.com)*.

MOTORBIKE, TRIKE & QUAD-BIKE TRIPS

Jandía is very close to nature and the peninsula is practically deserted away from the roads and still pretty much unspoilt. But be careful: most places here are a nature reserve, so going cross-country on your own can be expensive. Why not join a guided tour, which will take you to the most beautiful spots? Trips through the hills and dales of the area on dirt bikes and quads are offered by *Sahara Sports (tel. 669 79 71 62 | enduro-guru.com)*, while trike tours can be undertaken at *Xtreme (Av. del Saladar | at the CC Cosmo | tel. 928 87 56 30 | fuerte-trike.com)*. If you prefer an exciting off-road adventure, you can also book great buggy and quad tours there *(xtreme-car-rental.com)*. Scooters and quads are available at *Montes Quads (C/ Estrella del Mar | at the CC Faro | tel. 928 16 66 70)*.

SAILING & SURFING

The main provider for catamaran sailing, SUP and windsurfing in the area is the water sports centre on the beach side of the *Robinson Club (tel. 9 28 16 95 39)*. Below the *Club Aldiana, Surfers Island (tel. 928 16 63 49 | fuerteventura-surfen.de)* not only offers windsurfing, SUP and catamaran sailing but also surfing (rental and courses).

SEGWAYS

Get on a pair of electric wheels for a guided tour at *Senda Ventura (east of the town between Iberostar and Club Aldiana | tel. 638 67 95 04 | segway-fuerteventura.de/en)*.

SCUBA DIVING

The *Fuerteventura Buceo* diving school *(CC Cosmo, planta 1 | tel. 928 54 14 18 | fuerteventurabuceo.com)* has taken up residence at CC Cosmo. Manager Niko will take you by boat to the best diving spots around the island.

TENNIS

The better hotels offer artificial grass and clay courts. Lessons at *Matchpoint Sports (tel. 928 54 43 07 | matchpoint-world.com)*.

BEACHES

Four kilometres: that's how far you can stroll along the sunshine yellow sand of *Playa de Matorral*. From the old centre of the village head around the southern cape with the lighthouse until you have to climb over the first rocky outcrop with boulders. Two loungers and an umbrella will cost you 13.50 euros per day. There are five *chiringuitos* (beach bars) with hot food, plus showers, changing rooms and toilets. If you want to walk further, to Esquinzo, maybe, or even further to Playa Barca, watch out for the tides: The only comfortable way around the rocky outcrops is at low tide. It's best to start walking when the tide is going out and the sand isn't so trampled.

NIGHTLIFE

The best way to kick off your evening is with a sundowner and a sea view on the promenade down in Morro Jable. Try *Waikiki (Av. Tomás Grau Gurrea 27)*. Keep an ear out for live music, too. Two good places are in Morro, just metres from the promenade. Musicians play regularly on the terrace at *Canaima Bistro (closed Tue, Wed, C/ San Miguel*

ALTERNATIVE PLACE NAMES

Something as official as a place name should be constant, one would think. This is not the case on Fuerteventura. Instead of Morro Jable one can also say Morro del Jable, you can say Vega de Río de las Palmas or Vega de Río Palma. The holiday resort in the bay Caleta de Fuste completely confuses with several different names, such as Costa Caleta, Playa de Castillo, Castillo de Fuste or El Castillo... Many places have an article in front of the name such as La Antigua or La Oliva, but it is often simply omitted. There are no set rules as to which version should be used when.

7) on the other side of the *barranco*. They also serve cheap Venezuelan tapas and other delights for hungry guests or, since the musicians play outside, you can listen for free without sitting in the bistro. The cosy *San Borondón (daily | C/ Piragua)* is a meeting point for Spanish locals and tourists alike, who come to see the guitar-playing duo Jorge & José, watch the occasional karaoke singer or the owner who takes out his own guitar. The best music – also free – is at the bar in the hotel Faro every Friday from 9.30pm. Everyone is welcome, not just guests.

California (at the Casa Atlántica taxi stand) also attracts guests with its well-mixed cocktails (including non-alcoholic ones) and gin-based long drinks. After a long break, the *Surf Inn* right at the top of CC Cosmo has been revived. It's not just cocktails and tapas on offer here and Saturdays often see live music. Local discos are usually short-lived here as dancing tends to stick to the club hotels.

AROUND MORRO JABLE/ JANDÍA PLAYA

5 PICO DE LA ZARZA ★

16km / 5–6 hrs (there and back on foot) from CC Ventura

Before the reward you have to endure a bit of torture: it's uphill for three hours, and what is more, you'll have to

get up early. Your destination: the Pico de la Zarza, also known as *Pico de Jandía*. At 807m it's the highest summit on the island, and it's only accessible on foot. The hike as such is not very difficult. Normal walking shoes should do. Once you have found the entrance point, you cannot get lost as the path has been walked many times and is easy to identify. When the summit is not surrounded by trade wind clouds, the view from the top is quite overwhelming. Increase your chances of a clear view by hiking up in the morning rather than the afternoon.

The starting point is the large roundabout at the Jandía Playa village entrance, where the country road meets the salt marsh. Take the wide road past *CC Ventura* and the hotel *Occidental Jandía Playa*. Just behind

A misty view from the summit of Pico de la Zarza

the hotel, you turn left and, after about 600m, turn right (uphill) into a cul-de-sac; 200m further on turn right onto a track. Now you only need to follow the track. At about 700m you will reach the fence that surrounds the summit area in order to keep out hungry goats. At this height the trade wind clouds provide enough precipitation so that protected plants thrive between the rocks. To protect these plants for the future, please ensure that you close the gate behind you. From here, a narrow, winding path leads steeply up to the ridge, follow the ridge to the right to reach the summit.

Under normal conditions and walking at a moderate pace, your hike should take about five hours. You should bear in mind that there is no food available along the way and, of course, take enough water with you. The winds are strong at the top so you should also take something warm to wear. Just as important is good sun protection (hat and sunscreen) because there is no shade. (map) C2

6 WESTERN CAPE & COFETE ★

40km / 90 mins (jeep) from Morro Jable to Cofete via the western cape

The extreme western tip of the island, the *Punta de Jandía*, is often falsely referred to as the south cape, when Morro Jable is clearly more southern. The trip to Punta de Jandía, over a dusty bumpy road is still a bit of an adventure – an off-road vehicle is the best option, but an off-road bus also runs twice a day. There are two destinations worth visiting here. The little fishing village *Puerto de la Cruz* ((map) A3), which has three pubs that all serve fresh seafood, although the

Mountain, beach and ocean near Cofete

Caletón has the nicest places to sit. There is an exhibition in the nearby lighthouse, which runs on solar energy, giving information about local marine life *(Tue–Sun 10.30am–5.30pm)*. On a clear day you can see Gran Canaria from here.

On the way to Cofete, the next stop, you'll cross Degollada de Agua Oveja – a pass with an impressive viewpoint. *Cofete* (*🕮 C2*) itself, the most remote town on the island, consists of a few houses and shacks that use their own generators for electricity and have no running water. The few remaining inhabitants live from goat farming and the tourists that visit the *Bar Cofete (€€)* for its fish soup. The main attraction, however, is *Villa Winter (casawinter.com)*, shrouded as it is in mystery. The villa's owner, Gustav Winter (1893–1971), came to Gran Canaria in 1926 as an engineer. In 1937 he leased the entire Jandía Peninsula with possible links to the German Reich's wish to establish a naval base with an airport on the Canary Islands as part of the so-called *Etappendienst*. However, this failed to materialise, not least because General Franco imposed neutrality on Spain during the Second World War, and Winter left the Canary Islands. He returned after 1946, when he turned the peninsula into an agricultural business (mainly tomato cultivation and cattle breeding), treating the local population little better than serfs. The villa that bears his name was built in 1947 but was never finished and certainly never inhabited by him (see also "Discovery Tours", p. 121).

WHERE TO STAY IN THE SOUTH

LOCATION, LOCATION, LOCATION!

There's no getting away from it, a stay at the *Coronado Beach Resort (El Sol 14 | Morro Jable | solitour.com | tel. 828 91 99 95 | €€–€€€)* will cost you a fair bit. But you'll get your money's worth: the location up to 30m above the sea with the corresponding panorama, luxury terraces, no traffic noise, a garden on the slope, swimming pool and gourmet restaurant (see Eating & drinking). And everything is top-quality – both inside and out. It's a dream! The 12 apartments vary in size and are priced accordingly.

Whether you can explore the inside of the villa is up to its current residents, but it can't hurt to ask!

To get properly acquainted with that Fuerte feeling of solitude, you can walk to Cofete on an old royal road *(camino real)*. Drive 3.2km from the harbour to *Gran Valle*, where you can walk from the car park (signposted: "Red de Caminos de Pájara"). Keep going straight up the valley. The track has been revamped and you cannot get lost. There and back should take about four hours, so take some snacks and water along. There is a wonderful view from the mountain saddle.

DISCOVERY TOURS

Want to get under the skin of the region? Then our discovery tours are the ideal guide – they provide advice on which sights to visit, tips on where to stop for that perfect holiday snap, a choice of the best places to eat and drink, and suggestions for fun activities.

1 FUERTEVENTURA AT A GLANCE

- Through the centre of the island: mountains, churches, coastline
- The most beautiful beaches and wildest cliffs

Morro Jable/Jandía Playa

Corralejo

→ 175km

9 hrs (approx. 3 hrs total driving time)

Costs: 55 euros for hire car (compact car) and petrol, plus approx. 50 euros per person for admission costs, lunch and dinner.
What to pack: sun protection, swimwear.

Mountain landscape near Pájara

> Tips: The return journey to Morro Jable is 120km (approx. 1¾ hrs). Avoid taking this tour on Sundays, Mondays or bank holidays to ensure that all the shops and restaurants are open but not too busy. Set off at 9am at the latest in summer and even earlier in winter.

BEACH PARADISE ON THE SOUTHERN TIP

The tour starts in the south of the island at ❶ Morro Jable/Jandía Playa ➤ p. 99. First, head to the spectacular lagoon in front of Playa Barca ➤ p. 96. You'll get the best view over the lagoon from a ❷ viewpoint near Risco del Paso, to the south of Playa Barca; to get there, *leave the motorway 700m from the El Salmo exit. Then drive back to the FV2 main road*, following it to Costa Calma. On the way, you will be dazzled by the whiteness of the sand on both sides of the road: the island's trade winds transport it cross country from the north-eastern coast of the peninsula down to the south. *Exit the motorway again at the next opportunity and follow the old country road through ❸ Costa Calma ➤ p. 90, with its luscious green palm trees. Turn off the large*

roundabout at the next slip road towards La Pared, taking a northwestern route along the Istmo de la Pared. On reaching ❹ La Pared ➤ p. 95 the landscape changes from sandy white to a red clay-grey. At the top of the pass below the Tablada mountain, stop the car at ❺ Mirador Sicasumbre to take the signposted path up the hill. The southwesterly view takes in the coastline while the desolate mountain landscape with its herds of goats stretches to the north and east. The place is famous among stargazers: on a clear night and without light pollution, the sky reveals its full glory. It's worth heading here again at night (avoid full moon) for a truly special experience.

INSIDER TIP
Stargazing without a telescope

PIRATE CAVES & BARBARY GROUND SQUIRRELS

Shortly before arriving in Pájara, take a detour to the left to ❻ Ajuy ➤ p. 71. This former fishing village with its dark sandy beach is the starting point for a gentle stroll to the nearby ancient lime kilns and "pirate caves". With its jagged cliffs and crashing waves, this offers you a different picture of Fuerteventura away from its sandy tourist beaches. Stop in ❼ Pájara ➤ p. 70 to visit its church with its Aztec-inspired main entrance. While there, take your first break of the day in La Fonda *(€)*, opposite the church. Now comes the most adventurous part of the tour *along a narrow road winding uphill to the mountain's massif*. When you reach the top, stop to take in the views. The area is home to barbary ground squirrels who beg for food. Try to stay hard-hearted as the squirrels are actually an invasive species and don't belong on the island. Continue another 1.9km to another viewpoint over what was once a reservoir and now covers the top of the Barranco de las Peñitas ➤ p. 75 which cuts into the valley below. Next go downhill to ❽ Vega de Río de las Palmas. The small chapel is the island's most popular destination for pilgrims. Well-hidden inland, set into a deep valley, is ❾ Betancuria ➤ p. 72, the island's most historical town. Two hours can be enjoyably spent here visiting the church as well as the multimedia show in Casa Santa María, where you can also enjoy a light meal. It is possibly the island's nicest restaurant, and it also sells cactus jams and handicrafts.

Follow the tight bends up the road to the ⑩ Mirador Morro Velosa ➤ p. 74 with its amazing panoramic view over the north of the island. *Now continue to Antigua, where you turn right onto the FV-20 and head out of the town towards La Corte and the airport (Aeropuerto).* The road takes you past fields of aloe vera. Take a left turn signposted to the island's capital/airport where after a few kilometres you will soon reach ⑪ Salinas del Carmen ➤ p. 82, the salt lakes and salt

museum. You'll need to spend at least half an hour here. *Drive past the golfing ranges of Caleta de Fustes and the airport until you reach the island's capital* ⑫ Puerto del Rosario ➤ p. 60. *Turn right at the first roundabout, along the seashore and harbour, and stop after just 900m.* At the tourist information office, located at the next major roundabout, you can pick up the leaflet "Puerto on foot", a guide to the city's many sculptures. Grab a refreshing ice cream at Kiss *(Av. 1° del Mayo)* ice-cream parlour. The last part of the journey to Corralejo continues to the volcanic landscape in the island's north. *You'll reach this region's main attraction from the south – or via Corralejo if the old coastal road is closed*: the white ⑬ shifting sand dunes of El Jable ➤ p. 42. To round off your tour, enjoy dinner and the sea view at El Anzuelo in ⑭ Corralejo ➤ p. 42 before heading home.

Salt is harvested in the traditional way at the Salinas del Carmen

❷ HIGH POINTS OF THE NORTH

➤ A stroll through the capital
➤ Dinner with a sunset view

Corralejo — Corralejo

140km — 10 hrs (3 hrs total driving time)

Costs: 50 euros for hire car (compact car) and petrol, approx. 50 euros per person for admission costs, snacks, lunch and dinner.

What to pack: Swimwear, good walking shoes.

Tips: Do not take this tour on Sundays, Mondays or bank holidays. Set off at 10am at the latest and even earlier in winter.

COMBINE BREAKFAST WITH A STROLL THROUGH TOWN

Start in ❶ Corralejo ➤ p. 42 and head to your first destination at ❷ Puerto del Rosario ➤ p. 60. A normal weekday morning is the perfect time to take a stroll around the island's capital. *Leave the FV-1 at the first exit and follow the signs to "Puerto".* When you reach the harbour promenade, you will see the tourist information pavilion on the roundabout with the large fountain decorated with sculptures. Here you can grab a map of the city. After wandering around the city, stop for brunch at El Perenquén, a pleasant spot with a view over the harbour.

❶ Corralejo

31km 30mins

❷ Puerto del Rosario

28.5km 35mins

Head out of the city on the FV-20 towards Antigua. After leaving Casillas del Angel, turn right towards Betancuria and, at the next roundabout, turn right again to Oliva. You are now on the FV-207 and soon your route takes a left-hand turn onto the access road FV-221 heading to Parcelas and Molinos. When you reach ❸ Puertito de los Molinos at the end of this road, you'll catch a glimpse of the island's wild west coast. This is the

❸ Puertito de los Molinos

smallest fishing village on Fuerteventura and it looks as if it could belong to another century. Affluent city dwellers have their weekend residences here. A footbridge at the end of the road leads you over a barranco filled with water all year round; a shrine with Mother and Child stands on a square in the village – this naïvely decorated folk art sculpture is from the fishermen in honour of their patron saint. The bar-restaurant **Casa Pon** *(€)* offers good refreshments and snacks as well as a splendid sea-view terrace. From the small car park at the entrance to the village or along the beach (which, unfortunately, is not really suitable for bathing), you

13.5km 1hr 10mins

will reach a path and steps heading south to a viewpoint on the cliffs. The sight of the waves crashing onto the barren westerly coastline is amazing.

FROM THE OUTDOOR MUSEUM TO THE SACRED MOUNTAIN

Head back to the FV-207, turn left to Tefía and after just after 1.25km you'll reach the ❹ Ecomuseo La Alcogida ➤ p. 65. The open-air museum's car park and visitor centre are on the left-hand side. Plan 90 minutes for the tour around the museum. *Then head further north through the scattered settlement of Tefia. Take a left onto the FV-10* where you'll soon spot the Montaña Quemada ➤ p. 59 with its statue of writer and philosopher Miguel de Unamuno. Soon after you'll reach Tindaya. The village is named after the red mountain to the north, the Montaña de Tindaya ➤ p. 58. Rather than climbing it (which is generally not permitted anyway), head right, up the winding road towards Vallebrón. The ❺ viewpoint above the pass offers a splendid panoramic view with the sacred mountain of the native Canarians in the distance.

❹ Ecomuseo La Alcogida

11km 15mins

❺ Viewpoint

7km 10mins

❻ La Oliva

23km 55mins

LAVA LAND

Your next stop is ❻ La Oliva ➤ p. 57. There is plenty to see here, in particular the magnificent fortress-style Casa de los Coroneles, the Kirche, the art gallery Centro de Arte and the grain museum Casa de la Cilla. *On the FV-10 to Cotillo take a small detour via Lajares* ➤ p. 55. Although the embroidery school has probably closed for the day by now, *make a point of taking the old road to Cotillo from the roundabout* through old fields covered in lava stone and enclosed with lava stone walls – an unusual landscape with a strange appeal. Lava absorbs moisture from the air, hence these fields.

Canarian home decor at Ecomuseo La Alcogida

Try to catch the sunset at the 7 Punta de Tostón ➤ p. 54, the most northwesterly point of the island. *To get there, take a right through Cotillo* ➤ p. 53. It doesn't matter if you arrive early: you can also enjoy the evening sunset from the harbour's fortress tower or even better from one of the sea-view restaurants. After a good meal, *head back to* 1 Corralejo *via Lajares*.

3 NATIVE CANARIANS & MAJOREROS

- Journey to the past
- Hike through a gorge in the shade of palms

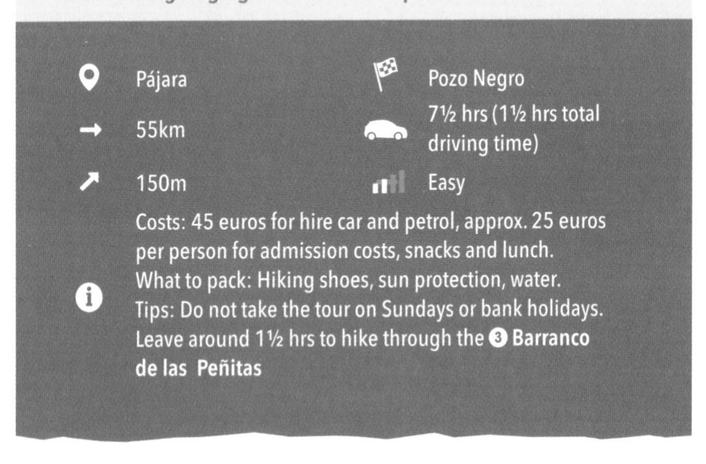

Pájara

Pozo Negro

55km

7½ hrs (1½ hrs total driving time)

150m

Easy

Costs: 45 euros for hire car and petrol, approx. 25 euros per person for admission costs, snacks and lunch.
What to pack: Hiking shoes, sun protection, water.
Tips: Do not take the tour on Sundays or bank holidays. Leave around 1½ hrs to hike through the **3 Barranco de las Peñitas**

1 Pájara
7km 13mins

2 Risco de las Peñas
6km 20mins

A GLIMPSE INTO THE PAST

Once you have reached 1 Pájara ➤ p. 70, *either from the south via La Pared or else from Tuineje*, you can dive straight into the island's history. First visit the Church, which will take you back over 300 years. Then take a coffee break in the country hotel Casa Isaítas (from the crossroads at the church, go 100m in the direction of Betancuria and it is on the left-hand side), since this is a traditional Canarian estate restored to its original style. *Now the tour takes you inland into the mountains. The next stop is* 2 Risco de las Peñas, a 426-m-high viewpoint. Your next viewpoint, the Mirador Las Peñitas,

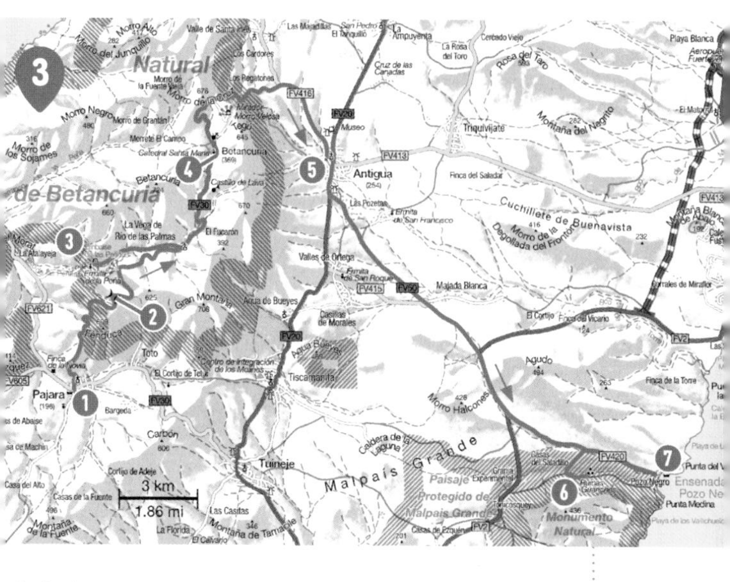

looks down onto a dried-up reservoir, the Barranco de las Peñitas (your next port of call – on foot). In the distance, you can spot a tiny white cube, the chapel of Ermita de la Peña. The journey continues downhill to Vega de Río de las Palmas ➤ p. 74. *When you reach the bottom, turn left (signposted: "Vega de Río Palma") and follow this small road for another 1.2km.* For the next stage of this trip you walk through the ❸ Barranco de las Peñitas ➤ p. 75, as mentioned above, until you reach the Casa de la Naturaleza. By now you deserve a bite to eat. Situated 120m in front of the bridge, this authentically renovated estate has been successfully converted into a museum and restaurant where you can relax and enjoy its splendid gardens, pond and traditional design.

❸ Barranco de las Peñitas
9.5km 1½hrs

Head back to the main road and turn left to ❹ Betancuria ➤ p. 72. Once the island's capital, this town is now the most popular inland destination with its monastery ruins, 400-year-old church, museums and an abundance of arts and crafts. Don't miss the multimedia show in the Casa Santa María as well as its exhibition and splendid garden. A visit to the

❹ Betancuria
10km 15mins

Fascinating mountains: viewpoint near Antigua

Archaeological Museum would also be appropriate on this cultural tour, provided it has finally reopened! Exhibits date back to pre-Hispanic times, more than 600 years ago.

THE ANCIENT CANARIANS & WHAT A CHEESE

⑤ Antigua
18km 30mins

A further 3km uphill and you will be welcomed by the colossal statues of the ancient rulers Guise and Ayose – as well as a fantastic panoramic view over the north of the island. The road now heads down to ⑤ Antigua ➤ p. 75. *Turn left at the church in Antigua and then left again onto the FV-20.* Head north and after a few hundred metres you can visit the cheese museum dominated by the old mill. Relatively speaking, the mill is not that old, but technologically it is already history. Exhibition room 1 takes you much further back in time to the formation of the Canary Islands, some 30 million years ago.

⑥ Atalayita

Now head back through Antigua and turn left onto the FV-50 airport-bound (Aeropuerto). Once you have left the suburb of La Corte, you'll drive past aloe vera fields and come to the FV-2. Turn right here and then exit this road almost immediately and head for Pozo Negro. After 3km, turn right to the native Canarian ruins of ⑥ Atalayita ➤ p. 77, the only point on the island that offers a glimpse into the lives of the ancient Canarians in precolonial times. The tour ends with a well-earned meal on a sea-view terrace of one of the fish restaurants in 7 Pozo Negro.

4 TO THE WESTERN CAPE & VILLA WINTER

➤ Jandía's Wild West
➤ A lonely villa shrouded in mystery

Start: Morro Jable/ Jandía Playa

Finish: Morro Jable/ Jandía Playa

Distance: 70km

Duration: 6 ½ hrs (total driving time 3 hrs)

Costs: 125 euros for hire car (jeep) and petrol plus approx. 15 euros per person for lunch

What to pack: Water and food

Tips: As some of the dirt roads on this tour require an off-road vehicle, it is essential that you hire a jeep. If you take a normal hire car, you will be in breach of the hire contract and will not be covered by your insurance.

OVER HILL & DALE IN A JEEP

First take the bypass road around 1 Morro Jable/Jandía Playa ➤ p. 99. *Shortly before you reach the port of Morro Jable, turn right onto the signposted track.* While the first section is surfaced, the rest of the way is a bumpy dirt track with just one stretch of tarmacked surface in the middle. This 20-km dirt road follows the coastline, separated from the shore by a stretch of deserted land dotted with just a few plants. Shortly before you reach the narrow peninsula of Punta de Jandía, with its lighthouse jutting out into the sea, you'll arrive in the unassuming village of 2 Puerto de la Cruz, which is a good spot for a break and bite to eat at El Caletón *(€-€€)* – it even has a sea view!

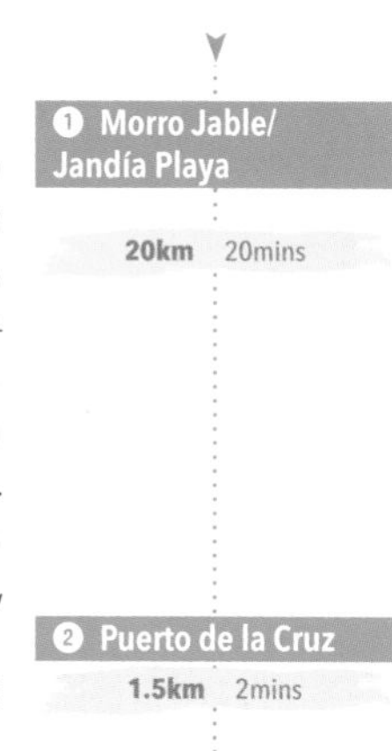

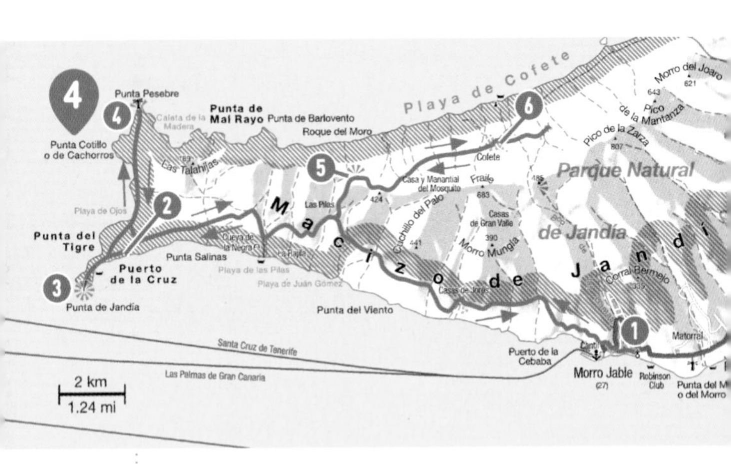

❸ **Punta de Jandía**
5.5km 5mins

In Puerto de la Cruz, you'll have to go off the beaten track to visit two must-see attractions. The first is the lighthouse at the most southwesterly point of Fuerteventura on the ❸ Punta de Jandía peninsula to the south of the village. Unfortunately, the small museum in the lighthouse does not have regular opening times. Back in Puerto de la Cruz opposite the Punta Jandía bar, *a tarmacked but potholed road takes you north to the nearby* ❹ Punta Pesebre. This is the most remote part of island which can be reached by car. On the way, you'll pass by an old runway on your right which was never in use.

❹ **Punta Pesebre**
14.5km 30mins

Now head back towards Morro Jable until you reach a crossroads, taking a left onto a mountain pass to the northern coast and Cofete. You will soon reach ❺ Degollada de Agua Oveja, and the most spectacular viewing platform on the island's southern coast. If you're driving with the windows open, take care that the wind does not blow anything out of the car or whisk your hat off! The light sandy beach of Playa de Cofete stretches out below you with the "small island" of El Islote at its easterly point. Beyond, you can see the vast beach of Playa de Barlovento, and on a clear day the northeasterly view extends all the way to the mountains at Pájara. From the beaches, the slopes stretch upwards to the 807-m-high Pico de Jandía (also known as Pico

❺ **Degollada de Agua Oveja**
5.5km 5mins

de la Zarza), the island's highest peak. Off this beaten track, you'll notice the towering *euphorbieae*, the long candelabra-shaped flowering plants that resemble cacti.

Shrouded in mystery: Villa Winter near Cofete

The next stop is 6 Cofete ➤ p. 107. Before reaching this seemingly forgotten settlement, you'll notice a two-storey building with a round tower standing alone on the hillside in front of you. This, the legendary Villa Winter, can only be reached by jeep or on foot. According to local legend, the German engineer Gustav Winter (1893–1971), who leased the whole of the Jandía Peninsula in 1937, used it as a submarine base for the German navy. By studying the archives and interviewing witnesses around at the time, two German residents on the island have proved that there is little evidence to support the legend or any of the other rumours circulating about this old villa. The building was never entirely finished and was never inhabited by Winter. However, under Franco, the entire peninsula belonged to "Don Gustavo", as he was commonly known on the island. Winter ruled over his enormous hacienda like a feudal lord. It was then divided into four parts which were all sold by 1964. Today the villa is inhabited and, although there are no regular organised visits, a small tip can usually open its doors to interested visitors. In Cofete, you can stop for a bite to eat in a simple pub before the journey home.

Resist the temptation to carry on along the endless sandy beaches; it is strictly forbidden to drive cross-country in this nature reserve and if caught, you will have to pay a hefty fine. *Instead, take the route back to* 1 Morro Jable/Jandía Playa.

GOOD TO KNOW

HOLIDAY BASICS

ARRIVAL

GETTING THERE

Plenty of budget and charter companies offer direct flights from the UK to Fuerteventura. With such a selection it is simply a matter of comparing prices and hunting for the best deal. In the UK, British Airways, Easyjet, Thomas Cook, Ryanair and TUI fly from London; there are also flights from other cities such as Manchester, Liverpool, Newcastle or Edinburgh. Most travel agents have very reasonable flat-rate package deals that include flight and accommodation. For people travelling from outside the UK the best option is to transfer at one of the major European airports, such as London or Madrid. Spain, France and the Netherlands also have direct flights on their national carriers.

There are a dozen daily flight connections to Las Palmas on Gran Canaria, up to four to Tenerife/Los Rodeos, and several times a week to Madrid. There are no connections to other Canary Islands. Bookings and information: *Binter (tel. 902 39 13 92 | binternet.com)*. For more flight information *tel. airport 902 40 47 04*.

Time zone

Fuerteventura is in the same time zone as the United Kingdom all year round (simultaneous switching to winter or summer time). The North American east coast is five hours behind GMT and the west coast is eight hours behind.

On arrival at Fuerteventura airport, transport to the holiday destinations is

Tiscamanita Windmill Museum

usually included in the package. Many car rental companies have counters at the airport and their cars can be c ollected at the numbered parking spots on the right (northern) end of the airport parking lot.

Fuerteventura has no direct ferry connections from mainland Spain. Coming from Cádiz, you have to travel via one of the other Canary Islands; connecting ferries run only once or twice a week. For two passengers with a car you can expect to pay at least 1,500 euros. Ferry information and reservations can be made at travel agents or directly at *trasmediterranea.es* or *navieraarmas.com*.

GETTING IN

If arriving from the UK, USA, Canada, Australia or New Zealand, your passport needs to have been issued less than 10 years before the date you enter the country (check the 'date of issue') and you must have at least 90 days on your passport after the day you plan to leave (check the 'expiry date'). Children will need their own passport.

CLIMATE & WHEN TO GO

Fuerteventura's season is year-round. However, the air and water temperatures are most pleasant in autumn. During midsummer, the sun and c onstant strong winds (flying sand on the beach!) can be unpleasant for small children and people with sensitive skin. From January to April it can be cool and the water temperatures are too cold for most people to swim. Always pack long trousers, a jacket and sweater in the winter and spring as the evenings can be chilly. Peak season prices usually apply to July/ August and Christmas. Note that many restaurants close in August.

GETTING AROUND

BUS

There are 17 bus lines that connect all the large towns. The lines most relevant to tourists are: lines 1 and 10 (Morro Jable/Costa Calma–capital, mostly hourly); line 3 (Caleta de Fustes–capital, mostly half-hourly); line 5 (Morro Jable–Costa Calma, mostly hourly); line 6 (Corralejo–capital, mostly half-hourly); line 7 (Cotillo–capital, three times daily); line 8 (Corralejo–Cotillo, mostly hourly); and line 25 (Morro Jable/Costa Calma–Oasis Park, mostly hourly). Lines 3 and 10 stop at the airport.

FERRY

Three ferry lines offer trips from Corralejo to Lanzarote/Playa Blanca daily; up to 16 crossings daily (travelling time 25–45 minutes, price per trip from 15 euros). *Líneas Fred Olsen (tel. 902 10 01 07 | fredolsen.es), Naviera Armas (tel. 902 45 65 00 | navieraarmas.com)* and *Líneas Romero (tel. 928 59 61 07 | lineasromero.com). Líneas Romero* is the slowest but also the cheapest.

INSIDER TIP More seafaring for less money

Fred Olsen and Naviera Armas also offer car ferries from Morro Jable to Las Palmas de Gran Canaria (three times daily, travel time from two hours) with connections to Tenerife.

RESPONSIBLE TRAVEL

Are you keen to keep an eye on your carbon footprint when travelling? Offset your emissions *(my-climate.org)*, plan an eco-friendly route *(routerank.com)* and pay attention to nature and culture. If you would like to find out more about ecotourism, please visit: *ecotourism.org*.

TAXI

The basic rate on weekdays 6am–10pm is 3.05 euros and 0.53 euros is added per kilometre; evenings and holidays 3.35 euros plus 0.60 euro per kilometre.

VEHICLE HIRE

An international license is not essential as national licenses are accepted. For more information about the traffic regulations see *canaryuk.com/driving.html*. You are required by law to wear a seatbelt and the speed limit for cars is 50kph in towns and 90kph on the country roads. The blood-alcohol limit is 0.25 and the Spanish police have zero tolerance; on Fuerteventura there are often roadblocks, especially at night and weekends.

There is a wide choice of rental cars available in the holiday resorts and at the airport. Three-day and weekly rates are the best. A small rental car starts at 130 euros per week; an off-road vehicle at about 70 euros per day. Ensure that unlimited mileage, collision damage waiver and full personal accident insurance are included in the

FESTIVALS & EVENTS

ALL YEAR ROUND

FIESTAS

Every town celebrates its patron saint day. The highlights are the fiestas *(verbenas)* which take place the weekend before or after the main date.

FEBRUARY/MARCH
★ ***Carnival:*** The majority of events take place in *Puerto del Rosario*. High point: the evening procession (Sat/Sun) (photo).

MARCH/APRIL
Semana Santa/Easter: Processions with images of Mary and Christ.

MAY
Tarajalejo (8); ***La Lajita*** (13)

MAY/JUNE
Corpus Christi (Puerto del Rosario): procession over "flower" carpets made from coloured stones.

JUNE
Lajares (13); ***Ajuy*** (24); ***Vallebrón*** (24); ***Las Playitas*** (29)

JULY
Pájara (2); ***Día de San Buenaventura*** (14) in Betancuria celebrates the conquest of the island; ***Fiesta Nuestra Señora del Carmen*** (16): the patron saint of fishermen is celebrated in Corralejo with a **boat procession**, similarly in Morro Jable.

AUGUST
Tetir (4); ***El Cotillo*** (around 22)

SEPTEMBER
Antigua (8); ***Vega de Río de las Palmas*** (3rd Sat): on the eve pilgrims cross the mountain to Vega Río Palma.

OCTOBER
La Oliva (7); ★ ***Fiesta Nuestra Señora del Rosario*** in Puerto del Rosario is the largest fiesta; ***Festival de St Miguel*** in Tuineje (13); ***La Ampuyenta*** (19)

NOVEMBER/DECEMBER
Tetir (30 Nov); ***Betancuria*** (8 Dec)

price. To hire a car the minimum age is 21 (23 for some companies). During the peak season you will need to book in advance. You do not need an off-road vehicle for normal travel around the island, but if you want to drive on the backroads or unpaved routes an off-road vehicle is recommended. Be aware that accidents or damage caused on unsurfaced roads is excluded from most insurance policies for normal rental cars. Irrespective of the matter of insurance, off-road jeeps are always recommended if you're planning tours to the westerly point and Cofete.

EMERGENCIES

CONSULATES

BRITISH CONSULATE ON FUERTEVENTURA

A British consular officer makes routine visits to Fuerteventura and is available for assistance and advice at: *Hotel Barcelo Corralejo Bay | Av. Grandes Playas 12 | Corralejo | La Oliva | 35660 Fuerteventura | tel. +34 902 10 93 56 | ukinspain.fco.gov.uk/en*

AMERICAN CONSULAR AGENCY IN LAS PALMAS

Edificio ARCA | C/ Los Martínez de Escobar 3 | 35007 Las Palmas | tel. +34 928 27 12 59 | es.usembassy.gov

EMERGENCY SERVICES

Dial *112* for police, ambulance and fire brigade. Or contact your hotel for help.

HEALTH

For a list of English-speaking doctors go to: www.gov.uk/government/publications/spain-list-of-medical-facilitiespractitioners and scroll down to "Gran Canaria, Lanzarote and Fuerteventura".

Chemists *(farmacias)* can be found in all the large holiday resorts and in Esquinzo, Puerto del Rosario and Gran Tarajal. Medication is often cheaper than at home.

ESSENTIALS

CAMPING

The official camping areas have no amenities (toilets, showers, water, etc.) and to use them you must register and pay a deposit in the local town hall. Maximum duration of stay in nature reserves is seven days; outside the official camping area 24 hours (permit required).

CUSTOMS

The Canary Islands have a special duty-free tax status but there are restrictions on goods you can take home with you. For tax and duty on goods brought to the UK from the EU go to *hmrc.gov.uk/customs/arriving/arrivingeu.htm*.

CYCLE PATHS

There are only 54km of paved cycle paths on the entire island, the rest of the signposted paths are off-road trails *(visitfuerteventura.es/rutas-ciclistas)*. Racing cyclists have to share most roads with cars. The older island roads are narrow and local drivers have little regard for cyclists.

HOW MUCH DOES IT COST?

Camel rides	*12 euros children 8 euros*
Beach lounger	*13.50 euros per day for two loungers with parasols*
Car hire	*from £60 euros for three days*
Windsurfing	*160 euros for a six-hour beginners' course*
Petrol	*1.40 euros per litre of regular*
Island tour	*50 euros with guide*

INFORMATION

For online information and to order brochures see: *spain.info/en_GB/*

SPANISH TOURIST BOARD OFFICES

In the UK:

6th floor | 64 North Row | London | W1K 7DE | tel. 020 7317 2011 | spain.info/en_GB

In the US:

60 East 42nd St | suite 53000 53rd floor | New York | tel. +1 21 2265 88 22 | spain.info/en_US/

TOURIST OFFICE

Patronato de Turismo | C/ Almirante Lallermand 1 | Puerto del Rosario | tel. 928 53 08 44 | visitfuerteventura.es/en

MONEY

Banks mostly open Monday–Friday 8.30am–2pm, Saturday 8.30am–12.30 or 1pm. You can draw money from ATMs using Visa, MasterCard, EC and debit card.

Major credit cards are accepted by many banks, hotels and car rental companies as well as in shops and restaurants.

NATIONAL HOLIDAYS

1 Jan	New Year's Day
6 Jan	Epiphany
March/April	Maundy Thursday, Good Friday
1 May	Labour Day
30 May	Canary Island's Day; Corpus Christi
25 July	St James' Day
15 Aug	Assumption
12 Oct	National Day of Spain
1 Nov	All Saints' Day
6 Dec	Constitution Day
8 Dec	Feast of the Immaculate Conception
25 Dec	Christmas Day

NUDISM

Nude bathing is taboo on local town and village beaches and in built-up areas but is commonplace and acceptable on many other beaches.

OPENING HOURS

Shops are usually open weekdays 9am–1pm and 5–8pm; in the holiday resorts they often also stay open at weekends. Restaurants often observe a siesta from 3–6pm.

POST

There are post offices in Corralejo, Costa Calma, Gran Tarajal and Morro Jable *(Mon–Sat until noon)* as well as in Puerto del Rosario *(Mon–Fri 8.30am–8.30pm, Sat 9.30am–1pm)*. Stamps are usually also available at hotel receptions; these stamps are from private postal companies so do not post your mail in the usual public letterboxes but hand them in at the same place where you purchased the stamps. Postcards and standard letters to the EU cost 1.35 euros.

PRICES

Prices on Fuerteventura are generally similar to those in the rest of Europe. A simple lunch in the most affordable restaurant is about 9 euros while a restaurant dinner will set you back 15 to 25 euros per person. There are no fees to access any of the beaches but you will need to pay if you want the use of deckchairs and umbrellas. Alcohol, tobacco and petrol are cheaper than at home.

TELEPHONE & WIFI

Classic internet cafés have virtually died out now. Many bars in all tourist towns offer free WiFi (just ask for the password). Most hotels now offer free WiFi to their guests but, especially in the larger resorts, connections are often really slow.

Dialling code to the UK: 0044, to the US: 001; to Spain: 0034. Your mobile phone will automatically choose a Spanish network.

Since Brexit, UK mobile phone users no longer receive free roaming in the EU by law. Most major networks have either reintroduced roaming costs, announced a date when roaming costs will return, or pledged to keep roaming free for their customers. Check with your provider before travelling. Some people choose to buy a Spanish SIM card or use Spanish phone cards called *teletarjetas*. International call shops, known in Spain as *locutorios*, are an option if you're calling outside Europe and WiFi and Skype are not available.

TIPPING

To tip waiters and taxi drivers, you can round up the bill by 5 per cent. For chambermaids 3 euros is recommended at the beginning and every four to five days thereafter depending on how happy you are with the service. For other services, small tips are also customary.

WATER

Drinking water is sold everywhere in plastic bottles or canisters. Although the tap water is safe, it comes mainly from desalination plants and should not be drunk in large quantities as it flushes minerals from the body.

Chunky cactus in La Oliva

WEATHER IN FUERTEVENTURA

High season
Low season

	JAN	FEB	MARCH	APRIL	MAY	JUNE	JULY	AUG	SEPT	OCT	NOV	DEC
Daytime temperatures	19°	19°	20°	21°	23°	24°	27°	27°	26°	24°	21°	19°
Night-time temperatures	12°	12°	13°	13°	15°	16°	18°	19°	18°	17°	15°	13°
Hours of sunshine per day	6	7	8	8	9	9	10	10	8	7	6	6
Rainfall days per month	3	2	1	1	1	0	0	0	0	1	3	3
Water temperature in °C	18°	18°	17°	17°	18°	20°	20°	21°	22°	22°	20°	19°

Hours of sunshine per day   Rainfall days per month   Water temperature in °C

WORDS & PHRASES IN SPANISH

SMALLTALK

yes/no/maybe	sí/no/quizás
please Thank you	por favor/gracias
Hello!/Goodbye/Bye	¡Hola!/¡Adiós!/¡Hasta luego!
Good day/evening/night	¡Buenos días!/¡Buenas tardes!/¡Buenas noches!
Excuse me/sorry!	¡Perdona!/¡Perdone!
May I?	¿Puedo ...?
Sorry?/Could you repeat?	¿Cómo dice?
My name is ...	Me llamo ...
What is your name? (formal/informal)	¿Cómo se llama usted?/ ¿Cómo te llamas?
I am from ... the UK/USA/Ireland	Soy de ... del Reino Unido/de los Estados Unidos/de Irlanda
I (don't) like this	Esto (no) me gusta.
I would like ... /Do you have ...?	Querría .../¿Tiene usted ...?

SYMBOLS

EATING & DRINKING

The menu, please!	¡El menú, por favor!
expensive/cheap/price	caro/barato/precio
Could you bring ... please?	¿Podría traerme ... por favor?
bottle/jug/glass	botella/jarra/vaso
knife/fork/spoon	cuchillo/tenedor/cuchara
salt/pepper/sugar	sal/pimienta/azúcar
vinegar/oil/milk/lemon	vinagre/aceite/leche/limón
cold/too salty/undercooked	frío/demasiado salado/sin hacer
with/without ice/fizz (in water)	con/sin hielo/gas
vegetarian/allergy	vegetariano/vegetariana/alergía
I would like to pay, please	Querría pagar, por favor.
bill/receipt/tip	cuenta/recibo/propina

MISCELLANEOUS

Where is ...?/Where are ...?	¿Dónde está ...? /¿Dónde están ...?
What time is it?	¿Qué hora es?
today/tomorrow/yesterday	hoy/mañana/ayer
How much is ...?	¿Cuánto cuesta ...?
Where can I get internet/WiFi?	¿Dónde encuentro un acceso a internet/wifi?
Help!/Look out!/Be careful!	¡Socorro!/¡Atención!/¡Cuidado!
pharmacy/drug store	farmacia/droguería
broken/it's not working	roto/no funciona
broken down/garage	avería/taller
Can I take photos here?	¿Podría fotografiar aquí?
open/closed/opening hours	abierto/cerrado/horario
entrance/exit	entrada/salida
toilets (women/men)	aseos (señoras/caballeros)
(not) drinking water	agua (no) potable
breakfast/B&B/all inclusive	desayuno/media pensión/pensión completa
car park/multi-storey car park	parking/garaje
I would like to hire ...	Querría alquilar ...
a car/a bike/a boat	un coche/una bicicleta/un barco
0/1/2/3/4/5/6/7/8/9/10/100/1000	cero/un, uno, una/dos/tres/cuatro/cinco/seis/siete/ocho/nueve/diez/cien, ciento/mil

HOLIDAY VIBES

FOR RELAXATION & CHILLING

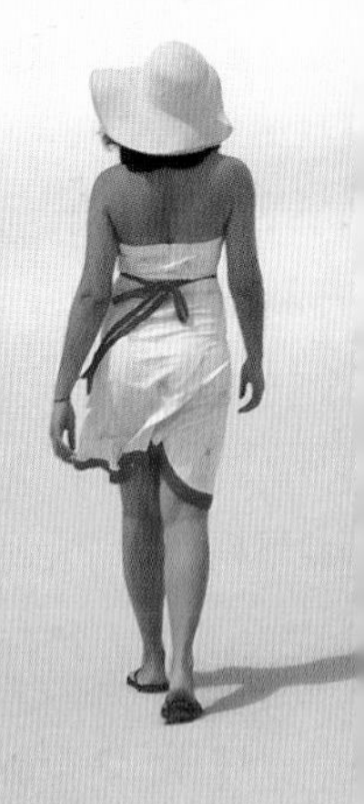

FOR BOOKWORMS & FILM BUFFS

THE HERMIT

This murder mystery is set on the island of Fuerteventura. Danish author Thomas Rydahl portrays an alternative image of the island paradise, where run-down bars and desolate beaches provide the backdrop for a dark tale of murder. After the body of a child is found in the boot of an abandoned car, a disaffected Danish resident – the hermit of the title – decides to track down the killer.

EXODUS: GODS & KINGS

Fuerteventura was used in the filming of Ridley Scott's 2014 biblical epic that brought the story of Moses to the big screen. Many of the island's inhabitants were employed as extras as well as hundreds of horses and camels. *exodusgodsandkings.com*

PLAYLIST

AÑATE – LA POLKITA

This Canarian folklore group from Tenerife perform on Fuerteventura from time to time.

AGRUPACIÓN FOLCLÓRICA DUNAS DE CORRALEJO – SEGUIDILLAS DE FUERTEVENTURA

Authentic dance and music traditions from the island; the group also tours.

The holiday soundtrack is available at **Spotify** under **MARCO POLO Canaries**

ALTHAY PÁEZ RAMOS – FOLÍAS SWING

This young timple virtuoso manages to elicit revolutionary tones and rhythms from this small guitar.

AITRA – FUERTEVENTURA

Fuerte inspired this Polish music producer to move into trance music.

FUERTEVENTURA EN MÚSICA

These videos from the music festival in Cotillo showcase where music is at on the island today.

Or scan the code with the Spotify app

EDDIE CHAN – FUERTEVENTURA MUSIC

Chan tops all the usual Fuerte travel videos with this funny YouTube video. Watch him surfing, quad biking and admiring the landscape.

UK.RADIO.NET/CITY/FUERTEVENTURA

Listen to five radio stations from Fuerteventura online: Can-And-More, Hola FM, Hola You 106.9 FM, Calima and Xtra Musica.

BEACH-INSPECTOR.COM/EN/DB/FUERTEVENTURA

Lots of detailed information about beaches, including in short videos. You can filter to find the beaches that match what you're looking for.

TRAVEL PURSUIT

THE MARCO POLO HOLIDAY QUIZ

Do you know your facts about Fuerteventura? Here you can test your knowledge of the little secrets and idiosyncrasies of the island and its people. You will find the correct answers below, with further details on pages 18 to 23 of this guide.

❶ How many goats supply the milk to make cheese on Fuerteventura?
a) 80,000
b) 8,000
c) 48,000

❷ When were the last volcanic eruptions?
a) in the 18th century
b) 2,000 years ago
c) 10,000 years ago

❸ Where did the pirates who raided the island in the 18th century come from?
a) England
b) Mauritania
c) Portugal

❹ Which animal species, now common on the island, has only been here a few decades?
a) rabbit
b) Barbary ground squirrel
c) raven

❺ What played a key role in the island's history?
a) a type of beetle
b) a type of mouse
c) a type of spider

❻ Which German chancellors holidayed here?
a) Kiesinger and Brandt
b) Schmidt and Schröder
c) Brandt and Kohl

Answers: 1a, 2c, 3a, 4b, 5a, 6c, 7c, 8b, 9b, 10a, 11c

Barbary ground squirrel

❼ **When Queen Sofía visited the island in 2009, she ...**
a) inaugurated the renovated Casa de los Coroneles
b) gave a speech to mark Fuerteventura's new status as a biosphere reserve
c) lent royal splendour to the release of baby turtles

❽ **A Majorero is ...**
a) a speciality made from gofio
b) a native islander
c) a local liqueur

❾ **Which of the following plants that grow on Fuerteventura does not come from America?**
a) prickly pear cactus
b) *columnar euphorbia*
c) agave

❿ **The nature reserves on the island have an area of ...**
a) 46km²
b) 65km²
c) There aren't any nature reserves here

⓫ **Jean de Béthencourt conquered the island ...**
a) after he was commissioned by the King of Spain
b) to kidnap a chief's daughter
c) with the subsequent blessing of the Pope

INDEX

WE WANT TO HEAR FROM YOU!

Did you have a great holiday? Is there something on your mind? Whatever it is, let us know! Whether you want to praise the guide, alert us to errors or give us a personal tip – MARCO POLO would be pleased to hear from you.
Please contact us by email:

sales@heartwoodpublishing.co.uk

We do everything we can to provide the very latest information for your trip. Nevertheless, despite all of our authors' thorough research, errors can creep in. MARCO POLO does not accept any liability for this.

PICTURE CREDITS
Cover photo: Esquinzo (stylefoto24/Shutterstock.com)
Photos: Corbis/JAI: Lubenow (117, DuMont Bildarchiv: S. Lubenow (9, 56, 95), O. Lumma (20, 123), H. Zaglitsch (8, 14/15, 23); f1online: Pritz (108); Getty Images/Cultura (10); huber-images: P. Canali (inner and outer cover flaps, 1, 43), M. Rellini (2/3, 120), M. Ripani (6/7), R. Schmid (51, 26/27, 99, 101, 124/125); Laif (82, Hilger (70); Look: Frei (74), A. T. Friedel (110/111), S. Lubenow (73), J. Richter (11, 60, 63); Look/age fotostock (27, 86/87); mauritius images: O. Lumma (24/25); mauritius images/Alamy (78, I. M. Butterfield (52), D. Dunbar (58/59), P. Greenhalgh (18/19), T. E. White (46); mauritius images/Alamy/CW Images (44); mauritius images/Alamy/Geogphotos (104); mauritius images/Alamy/Islandstock (92); mauritius images/Alamy/MARKA (Klappe hinten); mauritius images/Alamy/Travel stock44 (54/55, 77); mauritius images/foodcollection (28); mauritius images/Imagebroker (66/67); mauritius images/imagebroker (96/97); mauritius images/Imagebroker (136/137); mauritius images/image broker: Siepmann (31), Tack (49); mauritius images/Photononstop: P. Turpin (32/33); mauritius images/Science Photos Library (30); mauritius images/westend 61: M. Runkel (114), D. Simon (12/13); Norbert Eisele-Hein: N. Eisele-Hein (38/39); picture alliance: R. Hacken (85); picture alliance/Arco Images (35); D. Renckhoff (125); Schapowalow: P. Canali (134/135), R. Schmid (81); Schapowalow/SIME: P. Canali (91); H.-W. Schütte (139); vario images/image broker (64); VISUM: S. Boness (106/107); Shutterstock.com: MarVil (108), Peter Etchells (131)

4th Edition – fully revised and updated 2023
Worldwide Distribution: Heartwood Publishing Ltd, Bath, United Kingdom
www.heartwoodpublishing.co.uk

Author: Dr. Hans-Wilm Schütte
Editor: Jochen Schürmann
Picture editor: Ina-Marie Inderka
Cartography: © MAIRDUMONT, Ostfildern (pp. 36–37, 113, 116, 119, 122 inner flap, outer flap, pull-out map); ©MAIRDUMONT, Ostfildern, using data from OpenStreetMap, Licence CC-BY-SA 2.0 (pp. 40–41, 42, 61, 68–69, 88–89, 90, 100).
Cover design and pull-out map cover design: bilekjaeger_Kreativagentur with Zukunftswerkstatt, Stuttgart
Page design: Lucia Rojas

Heartwood Publishing credits:
Translated from the German by John Owen, John Sykes, Susan Jones and Suzanne Kirkbright
Editors: Felicity Laughton, Kate Michell, Sophie Blacksell Jones
Prepress: Summerlane Books, Bath
Printed in India

MARCO POLO AUTHOR
HANS-WILM SCHÜTTE
Hans-Wilm Schütte's inauspicious introduction to Fuerteventura back in 1990 involved sunburn. But that didn't stop him from falling in love with the island: its fresh air, beaches and barren mountainous landscape have lured him here time and again. A Sinologist by trade, Schütte now works as a freelance writer in Hamburg, but it is precisely as a contrast to his day job that he has come to appreciate "Fuerte" so greatly.

DOS & DON'TS

HOW TO AVOID SLIP-UPS & BLUNDERS

DON'T SWIM ON THE WEST COAST

Except for a few bays that are protected by reefs, the current along the west coast can be very strong and dangerous, especially if you lose your footing. Hardly a year goes by without someone drowning on this coast.

DON'T RISK SUNBURN

A long walk on the first day of your summer holiday (even when it is overcast and you're wearing a T-shirt) could give you a nasty sunburn. And at other times of the year, cool winds can make you forget just how powerful the sun's rays are. Always wear high-factor sunscreen, even when it is cloudy. Small children and those with sensitive skin are most at risk.

DO PACK WARM CLOTHES IN WINTER

Don't be tricked into thinking that Fuerteventura is always warm because of its location. In winter and early spring, the island is covered by a blanket of cloud, and temperatures do not rise above 20°C in the daytime and drop to 15°C degrees in the evenings, with a strong wind. Make sure you pack a warm jumper, windproof jacket, long trousers and warm socks.

DON'T DRIVE CROSS-COUNTRY

You should not take your vehicle off-road in any of the nature reserves, such as the Jandía Peninsula, or in the dunes of Corralejo. It is illegal and, if caught, you will be liable for a hefty fine.

DO TRAVEL BY JEEP TO COFETE

If you drive to Cofete in a normal rental car you will not be covered by the insurance. Off-road jeeps are always recommended for tours to the westerly point and Cofete.